The Tinned Tomatoes

Cookbook

Recipe notes

- Eggs are always medium (UK)/large (Aus/US).
- Butter is always unsalted.
- Herbs are always fresh, unless specified otherwise.
- Both metric and imperial measures are used in this book. Follow one set of measurements throughout, not a mixture, as they are not interchangeable.
- All spoon measurements are level, unless specified otherwise.
- Tablespoon measures: We have used 15ml (3 teaspoon) tablespoon measures.

Published in 2024 by Murdoch Books, an imprint of Allen & Unwin

Murdoch Books UK
Ormond House
26–27 Boswell Street
London WC1N 3JZ
Phone: +44 (0) 20 8785 5995
murdochbooks.co.uk
info@murdochbooks.co.uk

Murdoch Books Australia
Cammeraygal Country
83 Alexander Street
Crows Nest NSW 2065
Phone: +61 (0)2 8425 0100
murdochbooks.com.au
info@murdochbooks.com.au

For corporate orders and custom publishing, contact our business development team at salesenquiries@murdochbooks.com.au

Publisher: Céline Hughes
Project Editor: Lisa Pendreigh
Cover and Text Designer: Clare Skeats
Photographer: Mowie Kay
Food Stylist: Troy Willis
Prop Stylist: Max Robinson
Production Director, UK: Niccolò De Bianchi
Production Director, Australia: Lou Playfair

Text, design and photography
© Murdoch Books 2024

The moral right of the author has been asserted.

Murdoch Books Australia acknowledges the Traditional Owners of the Country on which we live and work. We pay our respects to all Aboriginal and Torres Strait Islander Elders, past and present.

ISBN 978 1 761500077

A catalogue record for this book is available from the British Library

A catalogue record for this book is available from the National Library of Australia

Colour reproduction by Born Group, London, UK

Printed by C&C Offset Printing Co. Ltd., China

10 9 8 7 6 5 4 3 2 1

MIX
Paper | Supporting
responsible forestry
FSC® C008047

SAMUEL GOLDSMITH

The Tinned Tomatoes

Cookbook

100 everyday recipes using the most versatile ingredient in your kitchen

murdoch books

London | Sydney

Contents

Introduction

If there's one ingredient that's always found in my kitchen cupboard it's a tin of tomatoes. They're like a reliable friend that you know will be there exactly when you need them. Their beauty is not only in their flavour and colour but also their versatility – there aren't many ingredients that you could write over a hundred recipes for without scraping the culinary barrel.

It's really no surprise that tinned tomatoes have become such a big part of our everyday cooking. The tomato is one of the most cultivated crops in the world and both the fresh and tinned varieties are evident in the cuisines of countries across all continents; from North African shakshuka to Italian pasta sauces to Indian curries to Brazilian stews. Tinned tomatoes allow you to create dishes all year round which incorporate one of the world's most loved ingredients.

Tinned tomatoes have a distinct flavour and concentrated aroma, which sets them apart from their fresh counterpart. Although not all tinned tomatoes are equal in their characteristics, depending on the variety used, processing methods and additives, they do share some general characteristics. Because tomatoes used for canning are harvested at their very peak ripeness, the natural sugars are captured and concentrated during processing. The natural acidity of tomatoes is also netted, which can add tanginess to dishes as well as brightening up sauces and stews. One of the reasons they improve the flavour of dishes so much is their umami notes, also known as the savoury flavour, thanks to the natural glutamates in tomatoes becoming concentrated during processing – this helps make dishes more flavoursome, complex and generally more appetising and delicious.

My cooking is very much that of a home cook; it's the type of food I enjoy eating as well as the food I get the most joy from cooking. It'll come as no surprise then that the recipes are divided into the following chapters: Storecupboard Saviours, Pasta Sauces, One-Pot Wonders, Family Feasts, Midweek Meals and Snacks, Sides and Sauces.

As we all increasingly look for convenient, time-saving and budget-friendly recipes, you'll see throughout the book that quick-cook recipes and dishes suitable for freezing are signposted using tomato-shaped icons. Likewise, those recipes that are vegetarian, vegan, gluten free and dairy free are clearly flagged. I've given options wherever possible for other flavour combinations or ways to use up leftovers. Many classic tinned tomato recipes go hand in hand with batch cooking – think spaghetti Bolognese (page 46) and chilli con carne (page 107), so consider making double quantities and freezing the extra; not only is this helpful for last-minute meals, but it also helps save energy and money.

Most of all, I hope that this book will not only illustrate just how versatile the tinned tomato is as an ingredient, but it will also be a source of inspiration when you've only got 5 minutes to find a recipe to cook that evening or when you've got friends coming round and you want a trusted recipe that you know will please everyone.

Varieties

The varieties of tomatoes we eat fresh are very different in style to those that are used for canning. When we buy tomatoes for eating raw in salads or as a snack we look for juicy, thin-skinned tomatoes that slice easily or can be burst with a bite. Most tomatoes that are processed are plum tomatoes, ideal because they have thick skins, plump flesh and are less juicy inside. Thankfully they're also intense in flavour, which is even further concentrated when put through the canning process. It's no surprise that many Mediterranean countries use tinned tomatoes for their sauces even when the fresh varietals are in season because eating fresh tomatoes just doesn't bring the same intensity of flavour.

Polpa Sometimes called finely chopped tomatoes, polpa are just that: tomatoes chopped so finely that they are like pulp. They're great for smoother sauces and hold up well to slow cooking. I find they are great for quick cooking, too, because they tend not to release lots of liquid so stay thick without the need to reduce them for a long time.

Chopped tomatoes The most used type in this book and their versatility has no doubt helped them become such a popular ingredient. They are great for stews, soups, sauces and even fresh in dishes like Pan con Tomate (page 160). As they're already pre-chopped they save time when cooking. They can also be found with additional ingredients such as garlic, chilli or dried mixed herbs already in the tin. Whole peeled tomatoes are chopped and processed.

Cherry tomatoes As the name suggests, they're the tinned version of the bite-size cherry tomato. Texture-wise, they tend to resemble their fresh selves more than other tinned varieties. Once a premium commodity, they're now available in budget supermarkets too so more accessible than they once were.

Whole peeled plum tomatoes The original tinned tomato. They're peeled while fresh then combined with tomato juice before being tinned. Though chopped tomatoes tend to replace them these days in sauces they're equally good and, if you're making a slow-cooked sauce, they'll break down during cooking and can be helped along by gently crushing them. Some people believe they have a better flavour than chopped so prefer to chop the whole version themselves. Great in stews, sauces or whole as part of a traditional English breakfast.

San Marzano tomatoes The emperor of the tinned tomato which has European protected designation of origin certification (P.D.P or D.O.P) meaning to get their certificate they must be grown in the Sarno valley and follow strict rules. In recent years, the US have begun to grow and tin their own, but these will not have the D.O.P certification. Because of their natural flavour, texture and low seed count, they're ideal for canning. Interestingly they are an heirloom variety, something that's become increasingly popular in the UK and the rest of Europe.

Tomato paste (concentrated purée)
Much more concentrated than your average tin of tomatoes, tomato paste has an intense flavour and is usually only used in small quantities (usually a tablespoon or two). It's often added to sauces to boost the tomato flavour just that little bit more.

Tomato passata (puréed tomatoes)
Great in sauces and bakes, passata is a thick tomato juice made by crushing fresh tomatoes. The skins and seeds are usually removed by passing the tomatoes through a sieve (strainer) – passata comes from the Italian word 'passare', meaning to go through – but some brands finely blend the skins and seeds before mixing them back in and heating to over 90°C/195°F. This gives the more concentrated passata a vibrant colour and great texture. It can be used as a sauce on pizza bases. Passata is also known as tomato purée.

Why use tinned tomatoes?

The process of canning has been around for over 200 years with Frenchman Nicolas Appert first hermetically sealing food for Napoleon's army and navy to help preserve the tomato for the journey. Initially preservation was in bottles and jars, but Englishman Peter Durand moved to tins for the Royal Navy a few years later finding tins lighter and easier to transport.

Processed foods are often thought of negatively and, while this may be true for some, the canning of tomatoes is actually considered to have a positive effect. The champion tomato nutrient is lycopene, a carotenoid which gives the tomato its colour. When heated, the concentration of lycopene – a powerful antioxidant – actually increases, so the canning process has a beneficial effect on the tomato.

When tomatoes are canned, they're often processed while incredibly ripe and still fresh, so the flavour is at its best. For the user this means that the intensity of the tomato flavour is a very pleasurable experience.

Not all tinned tomatoes are equal, however. My main rules when purchasing tinned tomatoes are firstly, pick the right type for what you're cooking and secondly, buy the best you can afford. If you can, buy the ones with the fewest ingredients and additives – usually just peeled tomatoes and tomato juice. When cooking dishes with very few ingredients where the tomato is the star of the show, it's more important to buy higher quality tins; when it's more of a base to a more complex or slow-cooked sauce, for example, you can get away with a cheaper tin as the deep flavours will mask any acidity.

Key to recipe symbols

 suitable for batch cooking

 suitable for freezing

 vegetarian

 vegan

 gluten free

 dairy free

Storecupboard
Saviours

Easy Shakshuka

Brunch, the new normal, still feels quite modern to me, even though it's said to be almost 150 years old. Shakshuka is a classic brunch dish; it's been modernised over the years to include more readily available ingredients. Originating in North Africa, this version is closer to the shakshuka you'd expect to find in your local brunch spot with a few tweaks to make it easy to cook at 10am on a Sunday when you're recovering from one too many tequilas.

SERVES 2

1 tablespoon olive oil
1 red onion, finely chopped
2 roasted red (bell) peppers, either from
    a jar or roasted at home and sliced
2 garlic cloves, crushed or finely chopped
Small bunch of coriander (cilantro), leaves
    and stalks separated, both chopped
1 tablespoon sweet smoked paprika
1 teaspoon ground cumin
½ teaspoon dried mixed herbs
Pinch of chilli flakes (optional)
1 × 400-g (14-oz) tin chopped tomatoes
1 tablespoon tomato paste
    (concentrated purée)
4 eggs
Salt and freshly ground black pepper

TO SERVE
Thick slices of sourdough toast or crusty
    bread (optional)

Heat the olive oil in a frying pan (skillet) with a lid over a medium-low heat. Add the onion and fry until soft, around 8–10 minutes.

Stir in the red peppers, garlic and coriander stalks and cook for 1–2 minutes, stirring, before adding the paprika, ground cumin, dried mixed herbs and chilli flakes, if using. Cook for 1 minute, being careful that the spices don't burn.

Stir in the tinned tomatoes, tomato paste and a good seasoning of salt and freshly ground black pepper and cook for 5 minutes.

Make 4 wells in the tomato mixture. Crack an egg into each one. (You can crack the egg into a cup or glass first, if that's easier for you.) Put the lid on the pan and simmer gently for 6–8 minutes until the eggs are cooked to your liking.

Serve the shakshuka with the coriander leaves scattered on top and with slices of sourdough toast or crusty bread alongside for dipping into the sauce, if you like.

Storage You can store the sauce for this shakshuka in the fridge for a few days or keep it in the freezer for up to 3 months. When ready to serve, defrost the sauce if frozen and reheat it until piping hot throughout, then crack in the eggs and cook as instructed above.

Cherry Tomato Orzo

Whenever I cook with orzo, I feel like I'm using some uber-modern hybrid of pasta and rice. Of course, it's not a modern ingredient at all. Great for speedy dinners, orzo cooks so quickly. Once you've mastered it, play with the ingredients and swap things out for your favourites. Here, the tin of tomatoes is the most important element, providing the base and colour to the sauce.

SERVES 4

1 tablespoon olive oil
1 onion, finely chopped
A few sprigs of basil, leaves and stalks
    separated
1 red (bell) pepper, chopped
3 garlic cloves, crushed
1 × 400-g (14-oz) tin cherry tomatoes
    or chopped tomatoes
500g (1lb 2oz) orzo
900ml (30fl oz) vegetable stock or
    chicken stock
Salt and freshly ground black pepper
Parmesan or vegetarian Italian hard
    cheese, grated (shredded), to serve

Heat the oil in a large, non-stick saucepan or frying pan (skillet) with a lid. Add the onion and fry until soft and beginning to brown, around 8–10 minutes. Chop the basil stalks while the onion cooks, then tip these into the pan along with the red pepper. Cook for around 5 minutes or until softened.

Stir in the garlic, cook for 1 minute then pour in the tinned tomatoes, orzo and stock. Season with salt and freshly ground black pepper and stir well. Bring to a simmer, pop on the lid and gently simmer for around 10 minutes or until the orzo is tender. Check every few minutes, stirring to prevent the orzo sticking. If the orzo needs more liquid, add a glug of hot water.

Tear the basil leaves into the pan and stir through the orzo. Serve with a scattering of Parmesan, if you like.

Variation: Chicken and Spinach Orzo Switch up the flavours by adding chicken and spinach. Add 400g (14oz) chopped chicken after frying the red (bell) pepper and cook for 8–10 minutes. Nestle in four blocks of defrosted frozen spinach or a few handfuls of fresh spinach a few minutes before the end of the cooking time. A couple of teaspoons of smoked paprika also works stirred in with the garlic.

Sausage and Loaded Veg Pasta

This makes a big pan of food, great for those days when you've got a lot of hungry mouths to feed or you just want to gorge on pasta. Personally, I love these kinds of dishes because I can eat loads and there will still be enough left to eat cold for lunch the next day. My best tip for cooking dishes like this is to make sure the veggies are properly cooked – especially the courgettes (zucchini) and mushrooms – so that they're golden and not soggy.

SERVES 4–6

350g (12oz) dried pasta (rigatoni works well)
1 head of broccoli (around 300g/10½oz), cut into florets
2 teaspoon olive oil
1 red onion, chopped
300g (10½oz) chestnut mushrooms, sliced
6 sausages, each cut into 4 pieces
2 garlic cloves, crushed
2 courgettes (zucchini), halved lengthways and finely sliced
1 carrot (around 150g/5oz), grated (shredded)
1 red (bell) pepper or 2 roasted red (bell) peppers from a jar, chopped
1 × 400-g (14-oz) tin chopped tomatoes
1 tablespoon dried mixed herbs
2 teaspoons paprika
Cheddar or Parmesan cheese, grated (shredded), to serve

Bring a very large saucepan of salted water to the boil. (At the end, everything is mixed together in the pan and so you do need to use a very large saucepan.) Add the pasta to the pan and boil for 6–8 minutes (or 2 minutes less than given in the packet instructions). Scatter in the broccoli and cook for a further 3 minutes. Scoop out a mug of the cooking water, set aside, then drain the pasta and broccoli.

Heat the oil in the same pan and fry the onion for around 5 minutes or until beginning to soften. Stir in the sliced mushrooms and fry for 5–8 minutes or until they've released their liquid and started to brown.

Tip in the sausage pieces and cook for a couple of minutes until browned. Add the garlic, cook for 1 minute, then stir in the courgettes, carrot and red pepper. At this point, I cook the veg for a good 10–15 minutes on a medium or medium-low heat and make sure it's all cooked properly.

Pour in the tinned tomatoes and scatter in the herbs and paprika. Stir to combine and cook for 5 minutes to heat through. Tip in the cooked pasta and broccoli and gently stir everything together. If it feels a little too dry, pour in some of the reserved cooking water – I always pour a little in anyway as it helps bring everything together. Cook for a few minutes just to make sure it's all hot and then serve. A scattering of Cheddar or Parmesan works nicely as a topping.

Make it fancy Got friends coming round and want to impress? For a pasta bake with a crunchy topping, scatter over some breadcrumbs and grated (shredded) Cheddar and bake in the oven at 180°C/160°C fan/350°F/gas 4 for 25–30 minutes.

Gnocchi with Tomato and Roasted Pepper Pesto

Quick to make and full of flavour, this gnocchi dish is a great midweek meal. You can, of course, play with the pesto, especially useful if you've already got an opened jar with just a few spoonfuls missing. Tomato and roasted red pepper are a classic match, with the herb and cheese elements of the pesto elevating this dish even further.

SERVES 4–6

2 teaspoons oil (olive, sunflower or vegetable oil are all fine)
1 onion, chopped
1 red (bell) pepper, chopped
1 × 400-g (14-oz) tin chopped tomatoes or plum tomatoes
1 × 200-g (7-oz) jar roasted pepper pesto
2 × 500-g (1lb 2-oz) packs ready-made gnocchi
Salt and freshly ground black pepper

TO SERVE

Cheddar, Parmesan or vegetarian Italian hard cheese, grated (shredded)
Handful of basil leaves

Heat the oil in a frying pan (skillet) over a medium heat. Add the onion and fry with a pinch of salt for 6–8 minutes or until softened and beginning to brown. Stir the red pepper into the onions and cook for a further 5 minutes.

Meanwhile, bring a large saucepan of water to the boil for the gnocchi.

Stir the tinned tomatoes and roasted pepper pesto into the onions and season with a little salt (the pesto will be quite salty) and plenty of freshly ground black pepper. Bring to a simmer and cook for 8–10 minutes over a gentle heat to thicken a little.

A few minutes before the sauce is ready, cook the gnocchi in the boiling water. Scoop out a mug of the cooking water, set aside, then drain the gnocchi. Combine the gnocchi with the sauce. Use the reserved cooking water to loosen the sauce as much as you like.

Serve the gnocchi with a scattering of Cheddar or Parmesan, if you like, and the basil leaves scattered on top.

Elevate it Especially good during the cold winter months, this dish can easily be transformed into a gnocchi bake. Scatter over a handful of breadcrumbs and some grated (shredded) Cheddar before baking in a preheated oven for 25–30 minutes at 200°C/180°C fan/390°F/gas 6.

Pizza, Your Way

There's one meal that will put a smile on pretty much everybody's face. Pizza.
If you're like me, you'll stick to the same toppings every time (my usual is
anchovy, capers and black olives, unless I'm on my hols and then it's seafood).
I can't help but feel it's because pizza is a comforting food that we all feel
safe with. This is the base on which to build your favourite pizza.

SERVES 2–4

2 × 25–30-cm (10–12-inch) pizza bases
   (either homemade following the recipe
   below or ready-made base)
Toppings of your choice, such as ham and
   pineapple; anchovies, capers and olives;
   cooked chicken and barbecue sauce
1 × 125-g (4½-oz) mozzarella ball, torn
100g (3½oz) Cheddar cheese, grated
   (shredded)

FOR THE PIZZA BASE

200g (7oz) strong white bread flour
200g (7oz) plain (all-purpose) flour
1 × 7-g (¼-oz) sachet fast-action yeast
1 teaspoon granulated white sugar
1 teaspoon salt
2 tablespoons olive oil

FOR THE PIZZA SAUCE

1 tablespoon olive oil
3 garlic cloves, finely grated (shredded)
1 × 400-g (14-oz) tin chopped tomatoes
2 teaspoons dried oregano

No pizza base, no problem
Fear not, you can use a baguette sliced
in half lengthways or even some crusty
bread slices. You can also try a flatbread
and treat it the same way you would a
standard pizza base.

First, prepare the pizza bases. If you're making your own
bases, sift together the strong white bread flour and plain
flour in a large bowl. Stir in the dried yeast, sugar, salt and
oil. Gradually pour in around 250ml (8½fl oz) lukewarm water
(you may need more or less) until the mixture comes together
to make a soft dough. Knead in a stand mixer for 5 minutes
using a dough hook or knead on a lightly floured surface
for around 10 minutes until you have a soft, elastic dough.
Put into a lightly oiled bowl and cover with a clean dish towel.
Leave in a warm place until doubled in size (around 1 hour)
then tip out onto a work surface, divide in half and create
2 equal-sized balls of dough. Leave to rise for a further
30 minutes on a baking tray, covered with a clean dish towel
again. Next, roll out each ball of dough to a pizza base shape.

If you're using fresh or frozen dough bases, prepare them
according to packet instructions.

Preheat the oven to 240°C/220°C fan/475°F/gas 9. Put two
large baking trays in the oven that are big enough to fit your
pizza bases on.

If you're making the pizza sauce, heat the oil in a frying pan
(skillet) over a low heat. Add the garlic and fry for a couple
of minutes or until softened. Tip in the tinned tomatoes and
scatter in the dried oregano. Cook for 10–15 minutes over a
medium-low heat to thicken the tomatoes. Leave to cool for
a few minutes then blend with a handheld stick (immersion)
blender if you prefer a smoother sauce.

Take the hot baking trays out of the oven. Lay a pizza base
on each tray then spoon the pizza sauce over the bases,
leaving a 2.5-cm (1-inch) border around the outside. Arrange
your choice of toppings on top of the sauce, then scatter
over the mozzarella and Cheddar.

Bake in the hot oven for 10–15 minutes or until the base
is golden and crispy and the cheese is bubbling and golden.

Tomato, Cheddar and Pesto Tart

Ready-rolled puff pastry is the saviour of impromptu dinner parties: it gives off showstopper vibes without taking too much time. Resist the temptation to pour the tinned tomatoes directly onto the cooked pastry: it's important to cook the tomatoes first to thicken the sauce, otherwise you'll end up with a soggy bottom. Use any pesto you like – most flavours complement tomatoes – but I prefer the classic Genovese basil pesto because, not only does it remind me of holidays in Liguria, the basil goes excellently with a tin of tomatoes.

SERVES 4–6

1 × 320-g (11-oz) packet ready-rolled puff pastry
1 teaspoon olive oil
½ red onion or 1 shallot, finely chopped
1 × 227-g (8-oz) tin chopped tomatoes
50g (1¾oz) Genovese basil pesto
40g (1½oz) Cheddar cheese, grated (shredded)
Handful of basil leaves, to serve

Preheat the oven to 200°C/180°C fan/390°F/gas 6.

Unroll the puff pastry sheet and lay it on a non-stick baking tray. Score along each side of the pastry, around 3cm (1 inch) in from the edge, so you have a scored rectangle just inside the pastry. Prick the inside of the rectangle all over with a fork. Bake in the hot oven for 10–15 minutes or until light golden brown and puffed up.

While the pastry cooks, heat the oil in a small pan. Add the onion and fry for 6–8 minutes or until beginning to brown. Pour in the tinned tomatoes and cook for a few minutes until thickened.

Remove the pastry from the oven and, using a spoon or fork, push the inner rectangle down so that you have a border of puffed-up pastry.

Pour the tomato sauce over the indented rectangle and gently spread it out to the border. Spoon blobs of the pesto all over the sauce and then scatter over the Cheddar.

Bake in the hot oven for 10–12 minutes or until the cheese is golden and the pastry is cooked through.

Mix it up If you're serving this at a gathering, it's easy to make a couple of different options. Try an alternative flavour like red onion chutney and goats' cheese to replace the basil pesto and Cheddar.

Cream of Tomato Soup

There's something incredibly rewarding about making your own soup. For me, it's the fact that you can make something really appetising with very little effort and you usually have some leftover for the freezer. Tomato soup is one of the nation's favourites and I love that something so full of nostalgia can be made so simply, with tinned tomatoes at its heart.

SERVES 4–6

2 tablespoons vegetable or
   sunflower oil
1 onion, chopped
1 carrot, chopped
1 celery stick, chopped
2 garlic cloves, crushed
2 × 400-g (14-oz) tin chopped or
   plum tomatoes
2 tablespoons tomato paste
   (concentrated purée)
750ml (25fl oz) vegetable or chicken
   stock (gluten-free, if necessary)
2 bay leaves
1 tablespoon soft light brown sugar
100–150ml (3½–5fl oz) single (pure)
   cream or whole (full-fat) milk

Heat the oil in a large saucepan with a lid over a medium-low heat. Add the onion, carrot and celery and fry with the lid on for 10–12 minutes or until soft but not golden. Stir through the garlic and cook for 1 minute.

Remove the lid and pour in the tinned tomatoes and squeeze in the tomato paste. Stir, then add in the remaining ingredients except the cream. Cook for 15–20 minutes until the mixture has reduced a little.

Take the pan off the heat. Remove the bay leaves, blend the soup well using a handheld stick (immersion) blender and return to the heat. Pour in 100ml (3½fl oz) of the cream, stir and taste. Add the rest of the cream, if you like. (I suggest 100–150ml/3½–5fl oz because a small pot of cream is 150ml/5fl oz and I prefer not to waste it, but it's best to taste the soup first.) Cook for 2 minutes before serving.

Storage You can store this soup in the fridge for a few days or keep it in the freezer for up to 3 months. When ready to serve, defrost the soup if frozen, blend or whisk it until smooth and reheat it until piping hot throughout.

Tomato Risotto

Risotto is my go-to dinner party dish when I'm in a hurry or want to impress without effort. Using tinned tomatoes to add flavour makes it even more effortless; there's no need for lots of frying before you start or for roasting veg to stir in later. There's also the added bonus of a lovely bright colour.

SERVES 4

2 tablespoons olive oil
1 onion, finely chopped
2 garlic cloves, crushed or finely grated (shredded)
300g (10½oz) risotto rice
125ml (4½fl oz) white wine (optional)
1 × 400-g (14-oz) tin chopped tomatoes
1 teaspoon dried mixed herbs
650ml (22fl oz) vegetable or chicken stock (gluten-free, if necessary)
50g (1¾oz) butter
75g (2½oz) Parmesan or vegetarian Italian hard cheese, grated (shredded), plus a little optional extra to garnish (or use Cheddar, if you have no Parmesan in the fridge)
Salt and freshly ground black pepper
8–12 sage leaves, to serve (optional)

If you're including the sage leaf garnish, heat the oil in a frying pan (skillet). Fry the sage leaves for 30–60 seconds until they go crisp. Remove the leaves from the pan and set aside on some kitchen paper to drain any excess oil.

In the same pan and oil, fry the onion and garlic over a gentle heat for 6–8 minutes or until soft but not golden.

Tip in the risotto rice and fry for a few minutes until it begins to change colour and turns translucent at the edges.

Pour in the wine, if using, and simmer for 2–3 minutes or until almost all of it has been absorbed by the rice.

Tip in the tinned tomatoes and mixed herbs, then season well with salt and freshly ground black pepper. Cook for a few minutes to allow the liquid to be absorbed.

Add the stock a ladleful at a time, stirring continuously until absorbed. Continue until the rice is cooked, about 20–25 minutes. You may not need all the stock or you may need a little water if you run out.

Take the pan off the heat and stir in the butter and three-quarters of the Parmesan until melted. Taste to check the seasoning. You can add the remaining Parmesan, if you like.

Serve in bowls with a crack of black pepper, a scattering of Parmesan and the fried sage leaves, if using.

Using up leftovers: Arancini Leftover risotto is perfect for making arancini, the crunchy rice balls that are great as a starter or nibble. Quickly chill any leftover risotto, form it into golf ball-sized pieces, then coat first in flour, then in beaten egg and finally in breadcrumbs. Exact quantities will depend on the amount of leftovers, however, a good ballpark is 50g (1¾oz) flour, 1 egg and 150g (5½oz) breadcrumbs. Heat a pan one-third full of sunflower or vegetable oil to 180°C/350°F on a probe thermometer (or until a cube of bread browns in 1 minute). Cook the arancini for 10 minutes or until crisp and golden and the rice filling is piping hot all the way through. You may need to do this in batches. Remove the arancini from the pan and place on kitchen paper to drain any excess oil.

Easy Gazpacho

The perfect summer soup for serving alfresco, gazpacho has its origins in Spain. A soothing swig of this tomato-fuelled, chilled soup is the ideal antidote for the Spanish sun, especially in the height of summer. Like a fandango, the fresh flavours of the raw onion and garlic dance on your palate, sweetened by the tinned tomatoes and enlivened by the lemon juice and Tabasco. This really is a case of the result being more than the sum of its parts.

SERVES 2–4

1 × 400-g (14-oz) tin chopped tomatoes, plum tomatoes or 1 litre (34fl oz) tomato passata (puréed tomatoes)
1 small garlic clove, peeled
1 shallot, peeled and chopped
1 cucumber, chopped
1 red (bell) pepper, chopped
1 basil sprig
½ tablespoon red wine vinegar
1 tablespoon olive oil
200ml (7fl oz) cold vegetable stock
Juice of ½ lemon or to taste
½ teaspoon Tabasco or to taste
Salt and freshly ground black pepper
Handful of basil leaves, to serve

Blend the tomatoes, garlic, shallot, cucumber, red pepper and basil together in a food processor or using a handheld stick (immersion) blender until smooth. If you prefer a super smooth soup, tip the blended liquid into a sieve (strainer) resting over a bowl and leave for 1 hour for the liquid to drip through, leaving the pulp behind – you can speed this up by using a spoon to stir the liquid around in the sieve.

Stir in the red wine vinegar, olive oil and stock. Season with salt and freshly ground black pepper, then add the lemon juice and Tabasco to taste.

Chill the soup in the fridge for at least 1 hour. You can prepare this soup the day before and store in the fridge until ready to serve.

Serve in bowls, cups or glasses with a crack of black pepper and a few basil leaves.

Why not try Adding a dollop of pesto or a few snips of chives or other fresh herbs to serve.

Patatas Bravas

During a tour of Spain by train, my partner and I were repeatedly asked if we wanted 'chips' with our meals. We always said no because we assumed the waiting staff were only offering them to us because they thought it was something us Brits might like. However, on one occasion we were given no choice and a big bowl of 'chips' was brought to our table. Except these chips were patatas bravas. And we were thrilled.

SERVES 4 (TAPAS STYLE) OR 2 (AS A SIDE)

600g (1lb 5oz) Maris Piper potatoes, cut into cubes
5 tablespoons olive oil
1 onion, finely chopped
1 garlic clove, crushed or finely grated (shredded)
1 teaspoon sweet smoked paprika
1 teaspoon hot smoked paprika or ½ teaspoon hot chilli powder
1 × 227-g (8-oz) tin chopped tomatoes
1 tablespoon tomato paste (concentrated purée)
Salt and freshly ground black pepper
Handful of chopped parsley, to serve (optional)

Preheat the oven to 220°C/200°C fan/430°F/gas 7.

Tip the cubes of potato into a roasting tray (sheet pan) then drizzle over 3 tablespoons oil. Season well and toss to coat them ensuring they end up in a single layer. Roast in the preheated oven for 25 minutes, remove from the oven and toss before returning to the oven for a further 20–25 minutes until golden and crisp.

Meanwhile, heat the remaining oil in a frying pan (skillet) over a medium-low heat and fry the onions with a pinch of salt for 8–10 minutes until soft but not browned. Stir in the garlic and both paprikas and cook for 1 minute.

Tip in the tomatoes, squeeze in the tomato paste and season well with salt and freshly ground black pepper. Cook for 10 minutes on a medium heat until thickened a little. Set aside until needed.

Tip the potatoes onto a serving plate and pour over the tomato sauce (warm it up a little first, if you like). Scatter over the parsley, if using.

Holiday Pasta

This recipe was born out of that feeling you get when you turn up at your super-budget holiday rental and there's absolutely nothing in the cupboard, not a drizzle of oil or even a salt shaker. It's expensive to stock the cupboard for a short stay, so the key is to shop wisely. Here, I recommend using tuna in oil, so both the fish and oil can be used, and tinned tomatoes with mixed herbs.

SERVES 4

2 × 145-g (5-oz) tins tuna in oil
1 large onion, finely chopped
500g (1lb 2oz) dried pasta
1 small jar roasted red (bell) peppers,
  chopped (optional)
1 × 400-g (14-oz) tin chopped tomatoes
  with mixed herbs (if possible)
2 teaspoons dried mixed herbs
  (if using tomatoes without herbs)

Drain the tuna, reserving 2 tablespoons of oil from the tins.

Heat the oil in a frying pan (skillet) over a medium-low heat. Add the onion and fry for 8–10 minutes.

Cook the pasta according to the packet instructions, usually around 9–10 minutes.

Meanwhile, stir the roasted red peppers, if using, into the onions and cook for a few minutes before stirring in the tinned tomatoes, mixed herbs, if using, and the tuna. Cook for 5 minutes to thicken a little.

Drain the pasta, reserving a little of the pasta cooking water. Mix the sauce into the pasta with a splash or two of the reserved water.

Nan's Beef

When I asked my nan to share this recipe, I didn't tell her it would be featuring in a book for fear she'd say no. As it turned out, her reluctance to share was because she thought it couldn't really be called a recipe as it's so simple. She's got a point. However, it's a delicious midweek dinner that is similar to a goulash with a moreish, rich sauce. It also requires very little effort and, other than the beef, you've probably got it all in the cupboard already.

SERVES 4

2 teaspoons vegetable oil
400g (14oz) stewing steak, sliced thinly
2 onions, sliced
2 garlic cloves, crushed
1 × 400-g (14-oz) tin chopped tomatoes
2 beef stock cubes

TO SERVE
Plain cooked rice or boiled potatoes

Heat the oil in a frying pan (skillet) or large saucepan over a medium heat. Add the beef and fry to brown it all over. You may need to do this in batches, depending on the size of your pan. Remove the beef from the pan and transfer to a bowl, leaving the oil behind.

Tip the onions into the same pan and oil, then fry for around 10–12 minutes or until softened and a little golden.

Stir in the garlic and cook for 1 minute before tipping in the tinned tomatoes plus three-quarters of a tin of water and the stock cubes. Return the beef to the pan and simmer for 20–30 minutes or until the beef is tender and the sauce has thickened.

Serve with plain cooked rice or boiled potatoes.

Storage You can store this stew in the fridge for a few days or keep it in the freezer for up to 3 months. When ready to serve, defrost the stew if frozen and reheat it until piping hot throughout. It should reach 70°C/160°F on a probe thermometer.

Chicken and Lentil Casserole

It's surprising how much you can do with a handful of storecupboard ingredients. This is the perfect dish for when the cold nights roll in or you have a few friends coming round and can't do a full shop. Lentils bulk out the dish and complement both the tomatoes and chicken well. Serve with boiled potatoes or crusty bread to mop up the sauce.

SERVES 4

4 chicken legs
1 tablespoon sunflower or vegetable oil
2 onions, chopped or sliced
1 carrot, grated (shredded)
1 teaspoon ground cumin
2 teaspoons dried mixed herbs
½ tablespoon plain (all-purpose) flour
1 tablespoon tomato paste
  (concentrated purée)
125ml (4½fl oz) white wine or water
100g (3½oz) dried red lentils, rinsed
500ml (17fl oz) chicken stock
1 × 400-g (14-oz) tin chopped tomatoes
Salt and freshly ground black pepper

TO SERVE
Thick slices of crusty bread or boiled
  potatoes

Season the chicken legs with salt and pepper. Heat the oil in a large saucepan with a lid, add the chicken legs and fry all over to brown. Remove the chicken from the pan, leaving behind any juices and oils.

Tip the onions and carrot into the same pan and gently fry for 10–12 minutes to soften.

Stir in the ground cumin, mixed herbs, flour and tomato paste, then cook for 30 seconds – you should notice it becomes a little paste like.

Pour in the wine or water, cook for a few minutes then tip in the lentils, stock and tinned tomatoes. Bring to a simmer, cook for 10 minutes then add the chicken legs back in, pop the lid on and simmer for 35–45 minutes or until the lentils are tender and the chicken is cooked through.

Serve with slices of crusty bread or boiled potatoes, if you like.

Simple Chicken Tikka Masala

According to many a snap poll, chicken tikka masala is one of Britain's favourite meals. You can whip together my simple version of this popular curry in under 45 minutes. Although chicken tikka masala has its roots in Indian cuisine, it's believed to have originated in Britain thanks to the immigrant South Asian community. Feel free to serve the curry alongside all your favourite Indian accompaniments; I tend to go for plain rice and naan bread.

SERVES 4

1 tablespoon sunflower or vegetable oil
2 onions, chopped or sliced
2 garlic cloves, crushed or finely grated (shredded)
Thumb-sized piece of fresh root ginger, finely grated (shredded)
6 chicken thigh fillets or 3–4 chicken breasts, cut into bite-sized pieces
4 tablespoons tikka masala paste (gluten-free, if necessary)
1 × 400-g (14-oz) tin chopped tomatoes
1 tablespoon tomato paste (concentrated purée)
150ml (5fl oz) double (heavy) cream

TO SERVE

Plain cooked rice or naan bread (optional)
Your choice of chutneys
Handful of coriander (cilantro) (optional)

Heat the oil in a large frying pan (skillet) and fry the onions over a gentle heat for 10–12 minutes to soften. Stir in the garlic and ginger and cook for a further 1 minute before adding the chicken pieces and frying until they're beginning to brown.

Stir in the tikka masala paste, fry for a couple of minutes then pour in the tinned tomatoes, half a tin of water and the tomato paste. Cook for 15–20 minutes until the sauce has thickened and the chicken has cooked through.

Pour in the cream, bring to a simmer then remove the pan from the heat.

Scatter over the torn coriander, if using. Serve the curry with plain rice or naan bread and any chutneys on the side.

Storage You can store this curry in the fridge for a few days or keep it in the freezer for up to 3 months. If freezing, do not add the cream before storing. When ready to serve, defrost the curry if frozen, then reheat it until piping hot throughout. It should reach 70°C/160°F on a probe thermometer. Stir through the cream before serving.

Pasta Sauces

Basic Tomato Sauce

This simple sauce is great when you fancy something light in flavour. You can easily add flavourings, but there's something comforting about its purity.

SERVES 8

1 tablespoon olive oil
1 onion, finely diced
2 large garlic cloves, grated (shredded)
2 × 400-g (14-oz) tins chopped tomatoes
    or tomato passata (puréed tomatoes)
1 teaspoon soft light brown sugar
1 teaspoon red wine vinegar

TO SERVE
100g (3½oz) dried pasta per person

Heat the oil in a frying pan (skillet) over a medium-low heat. Add the onion and fry for 6–8 minutes or until softened. Stir in the garlic and fry for 1 minute. Tip in the tinned tomatoes or passata with the sugar and vinegar. Stir to combine and simmer gently for 25–30 minutes.

Meanwhile, in the last 10 minutes of the cooking time, cook the pasta according to the packet instructions.

Drain the pasta. Stir the sauce through the cooked pasta before serving.

Triple Tomato Sauce

I love the intensity of this sauce, which brings together three forms of tomato: fresh, tinned and sun-dried. It combines the tomatoes with ingredients that bring out their best side, namely red wine vinegar, garlic and dried mixed herbs.

SERVES 4

1 tablespoon olive oil
1 onion, finely diced
2 garlic cloves, grated (shredded)
4 vine tomatoes, chopped
12 sun-dried tomatoes, chopped
2 teaspoons dried mixed herbs
1 × 400-g (14-oz) tin chopped tomatoes
1 tablespoon red wine vinegar

TO SERVE
100g (3½oz) dried pasta per person

Heat the oil in a frying pan (skillet) over a medium-low heat. Add the onion and fry for 6–8 minutes or until softened. Stir in the garlic, cook for 1 minute. Add the vine tomatoes and cook for 10 minutes or until they begin to soften.

Stir in the chopped sun-dried tomatoes with any of their oil remaining on the cutting board. Sprinkle in the mixed herbs and pour in the tinned tomatoes. Swill out any remaining juices from the tin with a few tablespoons of water and pour into the pan. Lastly, add the vinegar. Cook for 15–20 minutes or until combined and the sauce has thickened a little.

Meanwhile, in the last 10 minutes of the cooking time, cook the pasta according to the packet instructions.

Drain the pasta. Stir the sauce through the cooked pasta before serving.

Tomato, Aubergine and 'Nduja Sauce

Although 'nduja paste is a relatively new ingredient to me, it's been gracing the kitchens of Calabria for much longer. A spoonful stirred through tomato sauce imparts a warming heat and a saltiness that brings aubergines (eggplants) to life. Other veg which work well here are courgettes (zucchini), red (bell) peppers and mushrooms – the classics that cosy up to tomatoes so easily.

SERVES 4

3 tablespoons olive oil
1 onion, finely sliced
1 aubergine (eggplant), chopped
2–3 tablespoons 'nduja paste (depending on how spicy you like it)
1 teaspoon smoked paprika
1 × 400-g (14-oz) tin chopped tomatoes
Freshly ground black pepper

TO SERVE

100g (3½oz) dried pasta per person

Heat 1 tablespoon oil in a saucepan or large frying pan (skillet) over a medium-low heat. Add the onion and fry for 8–10 minutes or until softened. Drizzle in the remaining oil, tip in the aubergine and fry for 10–12 minutes, stirring often, until beginning to brown.

Spoon in the 'nduja paste and sprinkle over the paprika, stir, then tip in the tinned tomatoes. Add a little water to the tin and swill out anything left over into the sauce. Season well with lots of freshly ground black pepper. Simmer for 15–20 minutes until the aubergine has softened and you have a chunky, spicy sauce.

Meanwhile, in the last 10 minutes of the cooking time, cook the pasta according to the packet instructions.

Drain the pasta. Stir the sauce through the cooked pasta before serving.

Mushroom, Chilli and Balsamic Sauce

Balsamic vinegar is a charming companion to tomatoes. Its sweetness brings out the tomato flavours and its deep colour enhances the bright red to make it feel rustic and warming. Mushrooms are a natural addition to a tomato sauce, especially when you're looking for something comforting. I like to serve this sauce with wholemeal fusilli.

SERVES 2

250g (9oz) mushrooms, sliced
1 tablespoon olive oil
1 red onion, finely chopped
1 red chilli, chopped (deseeded if you don't like it too spicy)
2 tablespoon balsamic vinegar
1 × 400-g (14-oz) tin chopped tomatoes

TO SERVE
100g (3½oz) dried pasta per person (fusilli works well)

Heat a dry frying pan (skillet) over a medium heat. Add the mushrooms and dry fry until they release their liquid. Let the liquid evaporate, then drizzle in the oil and fry until golden. This can take a good 15 minutes. Remove from the pan, leaving behind any oil, and set aside.

Tip in the onion and fry for a few minutes until beginning to soften and brown. Return the mushroom to the pan with the chilli and cook for 1 minute.

Stir in the balsamic vinegar and tinned tomatoes and simmer for 10 minutes until thickened.

Meanwhile, in the last 10 minutes of the cooking time, cook the pasta according to the packet instructions.

Drain the pasta. Stir the sauce through the cooked pasta before serving.

Jazz it up This sauce goes well with beef; try frying 200g (7oz) sliced steak with the onion. Spinach, red (bell) peppers and courgettes (zucchini) all work nicely here too.

Puttanesca Sauce

If you enjoy salty, zingy foods then you'll love this sauce –
the anchovies, capers and olives give this a real punch.

SERVES 4

6 anchovies in oil
2 tablespoons capers
100g (3½oz) pitted black olives
2 tablespoons olive oil
1 red onion, very finely chopped
3 garlic cloves, crushed or finely chopped
½ teaspoon chilli flakes
1 × 400-g (14-oz) tin chopped tomatoes

TO SERVE

100g (3½oz) dried spaghetti per person
Handful of parsley or basil leaves

Drain the anchovies, reserving 1 tablespoon of oil from
the tin. Roughly chop the anchovies, capers and olives.

Heat the olive oil and anchovy oil in a frying pan (skillet)
over a low heat. Add the red onion and fry for 8–10 minutes
or until softened.

Add the garlic and anchovies and fry for 1 minute before
stirring in the chilli flakes and cooking for 30 seconds.

Scatter in the olives and capers, then pour in the tinned
tomatoes. Simmer gently for 25–30 minutes or until the
sauce has reduced a little.

Meanwhile, in the last 10 minutes of the cooking time,
cook the spaghetti according to the packet instructions.

Drain the pasta. Stir the sauce through the cooked pasta.
Serve with the herbs scattered over.

Arrabbiata Sauce

The literal translation of 'arrabbiata' from Italian to English is 'angry'. This fiery
sauce is a great one to have in your repertoire as it can be easily made from
storecupboard ingredients. It's a good base that you can add any veg to.

SERVES 4

2 tablespoons olive oil
1 large garlic clove, crushed or finely
    grated (shredded)
1–2 red chillies, deseeded and very finely
    chopped
1 × 400-g (14-oz) can polpa tomatoes

TO SERVE

Your choice of pasta or meat

Heat the oil in a frying pan (skillet) over a low heat.
Add the garlic and chillies and fry for around 10 minutes.
They shouldn't brown, just allow the oil to infuse with
their flavours.

Stir the tinned tomatoes into the oil and cook for around
15 minutes so it thickens up a little.

If serving with pasta, cook the pasta according to the
packet instructions, usually around 9–10 minutes.

Drain the pasta. Stir the sauce through the cooked pasta.
Alternatively, serve the sauce spooned over meat.

Ragù

Ragù is one of the most useful dishes you can make using tinned tomatoes. I always make a large batch and divide it into portions so I can use it in lasagne or serve stirred through pasta or alongside a creamy polenta. My friend Lesley grew up in Italy and makes the best ragù. She says slow cooking is imperative for the best flavour. Lesley cooks her ragù for 24 hours, but I go for a more conservative 2 hours to save on energy and so it's not left unattended for too long. Feel free to experiment with a longer cook – you're unlikely to regret it.

SERVES 8

2 tablespoons olive oil
2 carrots, finely diced
2 onions, finely diced
2 celery sticks, finely diced
4 garlic cloves, crushed or finely grated (shredded)
800g–1kg (1lb 12oz–2lb 4oz) minced (ground) beef (2 packs, depending on their size)
4 thyme sprigs
4 rosemary sprigs
2 bay leaves
200ml (7fl oz) red wine
2 × 400-g (14-oz) tins chopped tomatoes or plum tomatoes
3 tablespoons tomato paste (concentrated purée)
500ml (17fl oz) beef stock (gluten-free, if necessary)

TO SERVE
Thick slices of garlic bread (optional)

Heat the oil in a very large saucepan over a gentle heat. Tip in the carrot, onion and celery, put the lid on and cook for 15 minutes, stirring occasionally until softened but not golden.

Stir in the garlic and cook for a further 1 minute before tipping in the minced (ground) beef. Break up the meat with a wooden spoon and gently fry until browned.

Stir in the herbs and red wine, then simmer for a few minutes. Tip in the tinned tomatoes, tomato paste and beef stock and simmer with the lid on for 1 hour, stirring occasionally. Remove the lid and simmer for a further 1 hour to allow the sauce to thicken a little.

At this point, you can store the ragù in suitable sized portions in the freezer for up to 3 months. Alternatively, you can serve the ragù with slices of garlic bread or however you prefer.

Slow cooker Rather than simmer the ragù on the hob (stovetop), you can transfer the ragù to a slow cooker and cook either on low for 7 hours or on high for 5 hours.

Spaghetti Bolognese

Spag bol, comfort food of dreams. I'm not going to get into the correct way to make a Bolognese sauce as I've watched enough of Stanley Tucci's travels around Italy to know it depends whereabouts in Italy you're standing. I make a classic soffritto and go from there. For the ultimate evening meal, serve some garlic bread alongside and enjoy a glass of wine, if there's one left in the bottle.

SERVES 4–6

2 tablespoons olive oil
1 large onion, very finely diced
2 carrots, very finely diced
2 celery stalks, very finely diced
200g (7oz) unsmoked bacon lardons
   or chopped unsmoked streaky bacon
4 garlic cloves, finely grated (shredded)
   or crushed
400–500g (14oz–1lb 2oz) minced
   (ground) beef
3 tablespoons tomato paste
   (concentrated purée)
2 teaspoons dried mixed herbs
125ml (4½fl oz) white wine
250ml (9fl oz) beef stock, made from
   1 stock cube or pot
1 × 400-g (14-oz) tin chopped tomatoes
   or plum tomatoes
2 bay leaves
1 rosemary sprig (optional)

TO SERVE

75–100g (2½–3½oz) dried spaghetti
   per person
25g (¾oz) Parmesan cheese, grated
   (shredded)

Heat the oil in a large, heavy-based saucepan with a lid over a low heat. Add the onion, carrot and celery and cook with the lid on for 10–12 minutes until soft but not golden. This is the soffritto – a classic base of many Italian dishes.

Remove the lid, tip in the bacon and cook for 5 minutes to brown all over – you might need to turn the heat up a little to get it going. Stir in the garlic and cook for 1 minute before adding the minced (ground) beef and cooking until browned.

Squeeze in the tomato paste, scatter in the herbs and stir. Pour in the white wine and cook for 2–3 minutes until the wine has reduced a little so the alcohol cooks off. Pour in the beef stock, tip in the tinned tomatoes and stir in the bay leaves. You can pop in the rosemary sprig (whole), if using, and cook for 20–30 minutes until the sauce has reduced and is beautifully thick.

At this point, turn the heat down to low to keep it warm. Cook the spaghetti according to the packet instructions.

Drain the spaghetti, tip it back into the pan and stir through a good few spoonfuls of the Bolognese sauce.

Divide the spaghetti between individual plates or pasta bowls, then pile more Bolognese sauce on top. Don't forget to pull out the rosemary sprig and bay leaves, of course. Serve with a good helping of freshly grated Parmesan.

Big it up As you're going to the trouble of making a batch of Bolognese, I recommend doubling it and freezing whatever is left over. Store the Bolognese in single portions or a family-size portion so you only have to take it out of the freezer the night before you need it. The Bolognese will store in the fridge for a few days or in the freezer for up to 3 months. To reheat, defrost if frozen and heat until piping hot (it should reach 70°C/160°F on a probe thermometer).

All'Amatriciana Sauce

This classic sauce traditionally uses guanciale, a cured meat made from pork cheek. I use pancetta as it's more accessible and still has the necessary fat.

SERVES 4

1 teaspoon olive oil
125g (4½oz) pancetta
1 small onion, finely chopped
1 garlic clove, finely grated (shredded)
¼–½ teaspoon chilli flakes
1 × 400-g (14-oz) tin chopped tomatoes
1 tablespoon tomato paste
   (concentrated purée)
Salt and freshly ground black pepper

TO SERVE

100g (3½oz) dried pasta per person
75g (2½oz) Pecorino, grated (shredded)

Heat the oil in a frying pan (skillet) over a medium heat. Add the pancetta and fry for 5 minutes or until the fat has melted.

Stir in the onion and fry for 6–8 minutes or until softened and beginning to brown. Stir in the garlic and chilli flakes and fry for 1 minute.

Pour in the tinned tomatoes and squeeze in the tomato paste. Season with a little salt and plenty of black pepper, then simmer for around 10 minutes to thicken a little.

Meanwhile, in the last 10 minutes of the cooking time, cook the pasta according to the packet instructions.

Drain the pasta, reserving a little of the cooking water. Stir the sauce into the cooked pasta with a splash or two of the reserved cooking water. Stir in the Pecorino, reserving a little to scatter over when serving.

Pesto alla Trapenese

A Sicilian twist on the classic Genovese basil pesto, this is a tomato-based pesto. Using tinned tomatoes means you can enjoy this sauce all year round.

SERVES 4

50g (1¾oz) blanched almonds
2 garlic cloves
Half a bunch of basil (around 15g/½oz)
75g (2½oz) Pecorino, chopped into pieces
1 × 227-g (8-oz) tin chopped tomatoes
75ml (2½fl oz) olive oil
Salt and freshly ground black pepper

TO SERVE

100g (3½oz) dried pasta per person

Toast the almonds in a dry frying pan (skillet) for a few minutes until lightly golden. Give the pan a shake every now and then, watching to ensure the almonds don't burn.

Put all the ingredients, including the almonds, into a food processor and blitz to a coarse paste. Season well with salt and freshly ground black pepper and briefly blitz again.

Cook the pasta according to the packet instructions.

Drain the pasta. Stir the pesto into the cooked pasta or use as you would any other pesto.

Pasta alla Vodka

I've no idea who came up with the idea of adding vodka to a tomato sauce served with pasta, but this sauce really is delicious. I read somewhere that pasta alla vodka peaked in the 1980s after being served in nightclubs across America. I really hope this is true because I love the thought of clubbers dressed in their finest fashion trying to stay clean while battling with this vibrant orange sauce.

SERVES 2

1 tablespoon olive oil
1 banana shallot, very finely chopped
2 garlic cloves, crushed
¼–½ teaspoon chilli flakes (depending on how spicy you like it)
1 × 227-g (8-oz) tin chopped tomatoes
2 tablespoons tomato paste (concentrated purée)
50ml (1¾fl oz) vodka
75ml (2½fl oz) double (heavy) cream
25g (¾oz) Parmesan or vegetarian Italian hard cheese, grated (shredded), plus extra to serve
Salt and freshly ground black pepper

TO SERVE
100g (3½oz) dried pasta per person (penne rigate or rigatoni work well)
Handful of torn basil leaves

Heat the oil in a pan over a medium-low heat. Add the shallot and fry for 6–8 minutes or until softened. Add the garlic and chilli and fry for 1 minute before stirring in the tinned tomatoes, tomato paste and vodka. Fry for 5 minutes before blitzing until smooth with a handheld stick (immersion) blender or in a blender and returning to the pan. Set aside.

Cook the pasta according to the packet instructions, usually around 8–10 minutes. Drain the pasta, reserving a mugful of the pasta cooking water.

Reheat the tomato sauce, pour in the cream and scatter in the Parmesan. Heat, stirring to melt the cheese, for 1 minute before adding in the cooked pasta, a good seasoning of salt and pepper and some of the reserved pasta water (usually around ½ cup) to form a glossy sauce. Stir for 1 minute.

Serve with extra Parmesan and the torn basil leaves.

Pasta alla Norma

Also known as pasta con le melanzane because of its abundance of aubergines (eggplant), this dish is traditionally served with ricotta salata, a salty ewe's milk cheese. For me, it's easier to use Parmesan or Pecorino as I've pretty much always got either (or both) in the fridge. Aubergines are great in a tomato sauce because you get the richness that the tinned tomatoes add along with a kind of meatiness which the aubergines bring to the table.

SERVES 4

2 aubergines (eggplant), around 500g (1lb 2oz), diced
1 teaspoon salt
4 tablespoons olive oil
1 onion, finely chopped
Half a bunch of basil (around 15g/½oz), leaves and stalks separated
2 large garlic cloves, crushed or finely chopped
1 tablespoon capers, chopped
½ tablespoon red wine vinegar
1 × 400-g (14-oz) tin chopped tomatoes

TO SERVE

100g (3½oz) dried pasta per person (spaghetti, penne or rigatoni all work well)
25g (¾oz) Parmesan, Pecorino or vegetarian or vegan Italian hard cheese, grated (shredded)

Put the aubergines in a colander, scatter over the salt and toss. Leave for 30 minutes to allow the aubergines to release some of their water content.

Meanwhile, heat 1 tablespoon oil in a large frying pan (skillet) over a low heat. Add the onion and fry for 10–12 minutes or until softened but not golden. Turn off the heat.

Return to the aubergines, give them a good shake and tip them onto a clean dish towel or kitchen paper. Gently dab the aubergines dry and set aside.

Put the frying pan with the onion back on a medium-low heat and add the remaining oil. Tip in the aubergines and cook for 10–15 minutes or until the aubergines have started to brown and have softened. You may need to turn up the heat a little after 5 minutes.

Tear the basil leaves and chop the stems and set both aside separately.

Stir through the garlic and basil stalks. Cook for 1 minute before scattering in the capers and drizzling in the red wine vinegar. Stir everything together then pour in the tinned tomatoes and cook for 15 minutes or until the aubergines start to break down a little bit. At this point, the sauce will be quite dry, but will loosen once you use it with pasta.

Meanwhile, in the last 10 minutes of the cooking time, cook the pasta according to the packet instructions.

Drain the pasta, reserving a mugful of the cooking water. Mix the sauce into the pasta and splash in half the reserved cooking water, adding more if it needs loosening further.

Stir through the basil leaves and serve with lots of freshly grated Parmesan, Pecorino or other cheese.

Pasta alla Caprese

This is, quite simply, a spin on the caprese salad. Tomatoes, mozzarella and basil are the Holy Trinity – so simple and yet, when combined at their freshest, they can't be beaten. For this pasta sauce, I swap out fresh tomatoes for the tinned variety because they work so well here. One of my favourite things about this sauce is how the mozzarella retains some of its stringiness, so when you pull at your pasta it will have a little spring.

SERVES 4

1 tablespoon olive oil
1 onion, finely chopped
1 garlic clove, crushed or finely grated (shredded)
Half a bunch of basil (around 15g/½oz), leaves and stalks separated, both chopped
1 × 400-g (14-oz) tin chopped tomatoes
1 tablespoon balsamic vinegar
1 × 125-g (4½-oz) mozzarella ball

TO SERVE

100g (3½oz) dried pasta per person

Heat the oil in a frying pan (skillet) over a gentle heat. Add the onions with a pinch of salt and fry for 8–10 minutes or until softened but not golden. Stir in the garlic and fry for 1 minute before tossing in the basil stalks and cooking for a further 1 minute.

Pour in the tinned tomatoes and balsamic vinegar then cook for 10 minutes to thicken slightly.

Meanwhile, cook the pasta according to the packet instructions, usually around 9–10 minutes.

Tear the mozzarella into the sauce, stir until melted and then fold through the basil leaves.

Drain the pasta, reserving a little of the pasta cooking water. Mix the sauce into the pasta with a splash or two of the reserved pasta water, if you like.

Serve straight away.

Syracuse Sauce

Like my favourite pizza, this sauce contains anchovies, capers and olives.
These flavours deliver a salty zing to Mediterranean-style veg. I love this sauce
folded through rigatoni, but it would also work well ladled over meats.

SERVES 4

1 aubergine (eggplant), diced
1 teaspoon salt
2 tablespoons olive oil
1 onion, chopped
2 garlic cloves, crushed or finely chopped
4 anchovies in oil
1 × 400-g (14-oz) tin chopped tomatoes
　or plum tomatoes
1 heaped tablespoon capers, chopped
50g (1¾oz) black olives, halved
2 roasted red (bell) peppers from a jar,
　chopped

TO SERVE

100g (3½oz) dried pasta per person
　(rigatoni works well)
Handful of torn basil leaves
25g (¾oz) Pecorino cheese, grated
　(shredded)

Put the aubergine in a colander, scatter over the salt and toss. Leave for 30 minutes to allow the aubergine to release some of its water content. Give the aubergine a good shake and tip onto a clean dish towel or kitchen paper. Gently dab the aubergine dry.

Heat the oil in a saucepan or large frying pan (skillet) over a medium heat. Add the aubergine and fry for 10–15 minutes or until browned – I like to make sure they're browned as much as possible, so they hold their shape a little better.

Tip in the onion and cook for 5 minutes. Add the garlic. Drain the anchovies, add them to the pan and fry for 1 minute.

Tip in the tomatoes, capers, olives and peppers. Add a little water (a couple of tablespoons is usually enough) to the tomato tin and swill out anything left over into the sauce. Bring the sauce to a simmer and cook for 10–15 minutes to thicken a little.

Meanwhile, in the last 10 minutes of the cooking time, cook the pasta according to the packet instructions.

Drain the pasta, reserving a little of the pasta cooking water. Mix the sauce into the pasta with a splash or two of the reserved pasta water, if you like.

Serve with the torn basil leaves and Pecorino cheese scattered on top.

Tomato, Courgette and Feta Sauce

As with many Mediterranean vegetables, courgettes (zucchini) go so well with tomatoes. I love the saltiness that feta brings, as well as dotting this sauce with pops of white that add visual interest. Whenever I fry courgettes, I scoop out the seeds first so they brown nicely without becoming mushy. The seeds then get stirred back in later on so that nothing goes to waste.

SERVES 4

2 courgettes (zucchini)
3 tablespoons olive oil
1 onion, chopped
1 tablespoon red wine vinegar
1 × 400-g (14-oz) tin chopped tomatoes
150g (5½oz) feta
Freshly ground black pepper

TO SERVE
100g (3½oz) dried pasta per person

Slice the courgettes in half lengthways, scoop out the seedy centre and set aside. Slice the rest of the courgettes into half moons.

Heat 2 tablespoons oil in a large frying pan (skillet) over a medium heat. Add the sliced courgettes and cook until beginning to brown. Drizzle in the remaining oil and stir in the onion. Cook for 6–8 minutes or until softened and lightly golden.

Stir in the vinegar, tinned tomatoes and the reserved courgette centres. Add a little water (a couple of tablespoons is usually enough) to the tin and swill out any juices left over into the sauce. Cook for 15–20 minutes to thicken the sauce and soften the courgettes.

Meanwhile, in the last 10 minutes of the cooking time, cook the pasta according to the packet instructions.

Crumble in 100g (3½oz) feta and stir to combine. Season with lots of black pepper before tasting – I tend not to salt the sauce because the feta is already high in salt. Add a little more feta if you like, but it's nice to keep back a little to crumble over the top at the end.

Drain the pasta, reserving a little of the pasta cooking water. Mix the sauce into the cooked pasta with a splash or two of the reserved pasta water, if you like.

Serve topped with the reserved feta crumbled over the top.

Pancetta, Chickpea and Rocket Sauce

Ideal for after work and when you have hungry mouths to feed, this is a perfect midweek dinner – it's quick, tasty and embraces comforting flavours. Pancetta, chickpeas (garbanzo beans) and rocket (arugula) all go brilliantly with tomatoes and the harissa adds a warming note that brings it all to life.

SERVES 4

1 teaspoon olive oil

1 red onion, finely chopped

125g (4½oz) pancetta, chopped

1–2 tablespoons rose harissa paste (depending on the brand and how hot you like it)

1 × 400-g (14-oz) tin chickpeas (garbanzo beans), drained

1 × 400-g (14-oz) tin chopped tomatoes

60g (2oz) rocket (arugula)

TO SERVE

100g (3½oz) dried pasta per person (casareccia works well)

Heat the oil in a frying pan (skillet) over a medium heat. Add the onion and fry for 6–8 minutes or until softened. Tip in the pancetta and fry for around 5 minutes or until the oils are released and the pancetta begins to brown.

Stir in the harissa paste, adjusting the amount to suit your spice levels, then cook for a couple of minutes. Tip in the chickpeas and tinned tomatoes, swilling the tomato tin with a little water and pouring that into the sauce. Gently simmer for 15–20 minutes to thicken a little and to warm the chickpeas through.

Meanwhile, in the last 10 minutes of the cooking time, cook the pasta according to the packet instructions.

Set a couple of handfuls of rocket to one side, then stir the rest of the leaves through the sauce until wilted.

Drain the pasta, reserving a little of the pasta cooking water. Mix the sauce into the pasta with a splash or two of the reserved pasta water, if you like.

Serve topped with the reserved rocket leaves.

A note on garlic I don't include garlic in this dish because I like the flavours of the pancetta and harissa, but if you're a garlic fiend then feel free to add it. Garlic and tomatoes are a perfect match, but sometimes it's nice to mix it up a little.

One-Pot Wonders

Chicken Taco-Style Rice Pot

All your favourite flavours of a chicken taco, but in one rice pot. Dishes like this are great for midweek dinners when you're exhausted after a long day at work but still need to feed the family. Most ingredients you'll likely have in the storecupboard or fridge, the rest you can grab from a local store or mini mart. If you struggle to find taco seasoning, fajita seasoning works well too.

SERVES 4

1 tablespoon sunflower or vegetable oil
1 onion, finely chopped
400g (14oz) skinless, boneless chicken breast, sliced
1 red (bell) pepper, chopped or sliced
1 × 25-g (¾-oz) sachet taco seasoning (or fajita seasoning)
150g (5½oz) long-grain rice
1 × 400-g (14-oz) tin chopped tomatoes
550ml (18½fl oz) vegetable or chicken stock
150g (5½oz) frozen sweetcorn kernels

TO SERVE

Spoonfuls of sour cream
50g (1¾oz) Cheddar cheese, finely grated (shredded)
Handful of chopped coriander (cilantro)

Heat the oil in a large frying pan (skillet) with a lid over a gentle heat. Add the onion and fry for 10–12 minutes or until softened but not golden.

Stir in the sliced chicken and cook for 5 minutes or until beginning to brown. Turn the heat up a little and stir in the red pepper. Cook for 5 minutes to soften then mix in the taco seasoning and cook for 30 seconds.

Stir in the rice to coat it in the oil and seasoning, then pour in the tinned tomatoes and stock. Bring to a simmer, pop on the lid and cook for 15–18 minutes or until the rice is just cooked and most of the liquid has been absorbed. Check on it every few minutes just to check the stock hasn't evaporated; if necessary, add a splash of water.

Stir in the frozen sweetcorn kernels and cook for a few more minutes.

Serve in bowls with a dollop of sour cream and a scattering of both grated cheese and chopped coriander.

Lamb, White Bean and Chorizo Stew

Just as certain vegetables happily pair with tomatoes, some meats complement them equally well. My favourite meat to snuggle into a tomato sauce is lamb. It's not a ground-breaking revelation, I know; it's a constant theme in Italian cuisine and many well-known Indian curries centre around this combination. This stew is comforting when the colder weather kicks in, but it's also a lovely option for spring lamb. Whenever I need to be frugal, I swap the lamb for some stewing beef. Serve with couscous or boiled potatoes.

SERVES 6–8

800g (1lb 12oz) lamb shoulder or neck, cut into large chunks
2 tablespoons olive oil
200g (7oz) cooking chorizo, roughly chopped
2 red onions, sliced
4 garlic cloves, finely chopped
1 tablespoon sweet smoked paprika
1 teaspoon ground cumin
150ml (5fl oz) white wine
2 × 400-g (14-oz) tins chopped tomatoes or plum tomatoes
1 tablespoon tomato paste (concentrated purée)
2 rosemary sprigs
2 bay leaves
250ml (9fl oz) lamb or chicken stock
2 tablespoons red wine vinegar
2 × 400-g (14-oz) tins cannellini beans, drained and rinsed
Salt and freshly ground black pepper

TO SERVE
50g (1¾oz) pine nuts, toasted (optional)
Handful of chopped parsley (optional)

Season the lamb with salt and pepper. Heat 1 tablespoon oil in a large pan with a lid over a medium heat. Working in batches, add the lamb and brown it all over. Remove from the pan and set aside.

Next, fry the chorizo in the same pan until brown all over and it has released its oil. Remove from the pan, leaving the oil behind, and set aside with the lamb.

Add the onions and remaining oil to the pan and fry over a medium heat for 8–10 minutes to soften. Stir in the garlic and cook for 1 minute. Sprinkle in the paprika and ground cumin and fry for 30 seconds, then pour in the wine and bring to a simmer. Add the tinned tomatoes, tomato paste, rosemary, bay leaves, stock and vinegar and stir to combine.

Return the lamb and chorizo to the pan, cover with the lid and cook for 1 hour 30 minutes or until the lamb is tender. Tip in the beans and cook for a further 25 minutes.

Immediately before serving, scatter the pine nuts and chopped parsley over the stew.

Chicken, Chorizo and Prawn Paella

Paella, the Spanish one-pot dish, is traditionally cooked over an open fire in the classic paella pan. Chorizo is a modern addition, coming to the fore as the dish moved around the world. The use of tinned tomatoes is also a relatively recent one, which adds both a depth of flavour and colour. Paella's vibrant yellow colour comes, traditionally, from saffron, the cost of which can make the dish less accessible. The joy of adding tomatoes is that you get a lovely, warming colour without breaking the bank.

SERVES 4–6

175g (6oz) cooking chorizo, chopped
400g (14oz) skinless, boneless chicken
    breast, chopped into bite-sized pieces
1 tablespoon olive oil
1 onion, finely chopped
1 red (bell) pepper, chopped
2 garlic cloves, crushed or finely grated
    (shredded)
2 teaspoons smoked paprika
250g (9oz) paella rice
1 × 400-g (14-oz) tin chopped tomatoes
1 chicken stock cube
150g (5½oz) prawns (shrimp)
175g (6oz) frozen peas
Salt and freshly ground black pepper

TO SERVE
Handful of chopped parsley
1 lemon, cut into wedges

Fry the chorizo in a large frying pan (skillet) or non-stick pan with a lid for a few minutes until its oils have been released and it's beginning to brown. Stir in the chicken pieces and fry again for a few minutes to brown the chicken. Remove the chicken and chorizo from the pan, leaving the oil behind, and set aside.

There should be a thin layer of oil on the base of the pan (around 1 tablespoon), if there's not then add a little more oil. Add the onion and red pepper and fry for 5 minutes or until softened and beginning to take on colour.

Stir in the garlic and cook for 1 minute. Next, add the paprika and cook for 30 seconds and then add the paella rice, cooked chicken and chorizo, tinned tomatoes and 1½ tins water. Crumble in the stock cube and stir to dissolve. Season with plenty of freshly ground black pepper and a little salt (the stock cube will add salt). Bring to a simmer, pop on the lid and simmer for 12–15 minutes or until the rice is just tender. Keep an eye on it in case you need to add a little more water. The water should pretty much all have been absorbed.

Stir in the prawns and peas and cook for a further few minutes until both the prawns and peas are cooked through.

Serve with a scattering of parsley and the lemon wedges on the side.

Seafood Paella

Paella is thought to have originally included rabbit, as well as chicken, but then fishermen adapted it by adding seafood, presumably from their daily catch.

SERVES 4–6

1 tablespoon olive oil
1 onion, finely chopped
2 garlic cloves, crushed or finely grated
   (shredded)
2 teaspoons smoked paprika
250g (9oz) paella rice
150ml (5fl oz) white wine
1 × 400-g (14-oz) tin chopped tomatoes
1 vegetable or fish stock cube
400g (14oz) firm white fish, such as cod,
   coley or pollock, cut into large chunks
150g (5½oz) live mussels
150g (5½oz) king prawns (jumbo shrimp)
175g (6oz) frozen peas
Salt and freshly ground black pepper

TO SERVE
Handful of chopped parsley
1 lemon, cut into wedges

Heat the oil in a large frying pan (skillet) with a lid over a medium-low heat and fry the onion for 10–12 minutes or until softened but not golden. Stir in the garlic and cook for 1 minute. Next, add the paprika and cook, stirring continuously, for 30 seconds.

Tip in the paella rice and cook for a few minutes until beginning to turn opaque at the edges. Pour in the wine and cook for a few minutes until the liquid has been absorbed and the alcohol has cooked off.

Pour in the tinned tomatoes and 1½ tins water, then crumble in the stock cube and stir to dissolve. Season with plenty of freshly ground black pepper and a little salt (the stock cube will add salt). Simmer for 8–10 minutes or until the rice is just tender. You may need to add a little more water, so keep an eye on it. The water should pretty much all have been absorbed.

Stir in the white fish and top with the mussels. Put the lid on the pan and cook for 10 minutes before scattering the prawns around the mussels. At this point you can also scatter over the peas. Cook for a few minutes until the rice and peas are cooked through.

Serve with a scattering of chopped parsley and lemon wedges for squeezing over.

Cod and Red Pepper Traybake

Cod is a great fish to use in a traybake because its firm texture means that it doesn't flake apart when you're scooping it out. If you keep some frozen cod fillets in the freezer then this dish is pretty much a storecupboard dish, too, with everything in most cupboards or easily purchased from a local store.

SERVES 4

1 large onion, chopped
2 red (bell) peppers, deseeded and
   chopped
4 garlic cloves, skin on
3 tablespoons olive oil
1 × 400-g (14-oz) tin chopped tomatoes
1 teaspoon dried mixed herbs
75g (2½oz) black olives, roughly chopped
   or halved
4 cod fillets or other firm white fish
Salt and freshly ground black pepper

TO SERVE
Handful of chopped parsley
1 lemon, cut into wedges
Sautéed potatoes or thick slices of crusty
   bread (optional)

Preheat the oven to 200°C/180°C fan/390°F/gas 6.

Put the onion, red peppers and garlic cloves into a roasting tin (sheet pan) and toss them in 2 tablespoons oil. Roast in the preheated oven for 15 minutes, then mix up the vegetables and return the tin to the oven to roast for a further 10–15 minutes or until soft and slightly golden.

Pour the tomatoes over the vegetables, then mix in the dried herbs and olives and season well. Roast in the oven for 5 minutes.

Lay the fish fillets on top of the vegetables, gently pushing them down into the tomato sauce. Drizzle the remaining oil onto the fish and season the fillets on top. Roast for 12–15 minutes or until the fish is cooked through.

Scatter over the chopped parsley. Serve with the lemon wedges to squeeze over and some sautéed potatoes or slices of crusty bread alongside, if you like.

Fish Stew

There's something both summery and comforting about a fish stew. The lightness of the fish and sauce make it easy to eat even during hot weather, but the comforting flavours of a fishy-tomato sauce lend themselves to the colder months too. Look for the MSC logo when buying fish to ensure it's as sustainable as possible. I haven't specified the type of fish to use here because this can change yearly depending on the health of the fish stocks.

SERVES 4–6

2 tablespoons olive oil
1 onion, chopped
1 celery stick, finely chopped
Half a small bunch of parsley, leaves and
   stalks separated, both chopped
2 garlic cloves, crushed or finely grated
   (shredded)
125ml (4½oz) white wine
1 × 400-g (14-oz) tin chopped tomatoes
500ml (17fl oz) fish stock
½ teaspoon Tabasco or to taste (optional)
250g (9oz) sustainable white fish,
   chopped into large chunks
400g (14oz) live mussels, scrubbed and
   debearded
150g (5½oz) sustainable raw shelled king
   prawns (jumbo shrimp)

TO SERVE
1 lemon, cut into wedges
Thick slices of crusty bread (optional)

Heat the oil in a large saucepan with a lid over a gentle heat. Add the onion, celery and parsley stalks and fry for 10–12 minutes or until they have softened. Stir in the garlic and cook for 1 minute.

Pour in the wine, cook for a few minutes to cook off the alcohol and then tip in the tinned tomatoes, fish stock and Tabasco, if using. Simmer gently for 5–10 minutes to thicken slightly.

Stir in the fish and cook for 3 minutes.

Discard any broken or open mussels (give them a flick first to see if they make any movement, if so it's fine). Add the mussels to the pan along with the prawns and give everything a stir. Cover the pan with the lid and cook for a further 3 minutes or until the mussels are cooked. Discard any unopened ones.

Scatter over the chopped parsley. Serve with lemon wedges for squeezing over and slices of crusty bread, if you like.

Flavour boost For a Spanish vibe, add 100g (3½oz) chopped chorizo at the same time as the garlic along with 1 teaspoon smoked paprika.

Mussels in Spicy Tomato Sauce

Mussels are a reasonably inexpensive protein, which are super-quick to cook and yet feel incredibly indulgent. You can swap out the 'nduja for a chopped red chilli, if you like, but I really do recommend the 'nduja as the flavour is amazing – smoky and spicy.

SERVES 2

½ tablespoon olive oil
2 banana shallots, finely chopped
1 garlic clove, crushed
2 tablespoons 'nduja paste or 1 red chilli,
  chopped
1 × 400-g (14-oz) tin chopped tomatoes
125ml (4½fl oz) white wine
1kg (2lb 4oz) live mussels, scrubbed and
  debearded

TO SERVE

Small handful of finely chopped parsley
French fries or thick slices of crusty
  bread (optional)

Heat the oil in a large saucepan with a lid over a medium heat. Add the shallots and fry for 4–5 minutes to soften before adding the garlic and frying for a further minute. Stir in the 'nduja and cook for a minute to release the flavours.

Pour in the tinned tomatoes and wine and then simmer for 5 minutes.

Discard any broken or open mussels (give them a flick first to see if they make any movement, if so it's fine). Add the mussels to the pan, give them a stir, pop on the lid and cook for 4–5 minutes or until the mussels are cooked. Discard any unopened ones.

Scatter over the chopped parsley and then stir. Serve with French fries or slices of crusty bread, if you prefer.

Sausage and Mozzarella Pasta Bake

While I stand by my Tuna Pasta Bake (page 136) being the holder of the best pasta bake award, sometimes you need a change. What better way to do that than with pasta enveloped in tomato and mozzarella with nuggets of sausage? If you're using a chorizo-style sausage then try adding some sun-dried tomatoes and paprika, whilst a pork and fennel sausage can be complemented with more veg, such as courgettes (zucchini) and mushrooms.

SERVES 4–6

400g (14oz) dried pasta (I use penne or rigatoni)
2 teaspoons sunflower or vegetable oil
1 onion, chopped
6 sausages, each cut into 4 pieces
2 red or yellow (bell) peppers, chopped
1 teaspoon dried mixed herbs
1 × 400-g (14-oz) tin chopped tomatoes
1 tablespoon tomato paste (concentrated purée)
2 teaspoons red wine vinegar
100g (3½oz) spinach (optional)
1 or 2 × 125-g (4½-oz) mozzarella balls (I usually use 1 × 125-g (4½-oz) mozzarella ball to serve 4)
2 basil sprigs, leaves picked and torn

FOR THE CRUMB TOPPING (OPTIONAL)

75g (2½oz) panko breadcrumbs
75g (2½oz) Cheddar cheese, grated (shredded)

Cook the pasta until al dente in a large ovenproof pan according to the packet instructions, about 8–10 minutes. Drain the pasta, reserving a mugful of the cooking water.

In the same pan, heat the oil and fry the onion with a pinch of salt until softened, around 6–8 minutes. Tip in the sausage pieces and fry for a few minutes until browned. Stir in the red peppers and cook for 5 minutes to soften a little. Mix in the herbs then follow with the tinned tomatoes, tomato paste and red wine vinegar. Stir everything together and then cook for 10 minutes over a medium-low heat.

Meanwhile, if you're making the crumb topping, combine the panko breadcrumbs and Cheddar and set aside.

Preheat the oven to 200°C/180°C fan/390°F/gas 6.

Mix the spinach into the sauce and cook for 2 minutes or until wilted. Turn off the heat. Return the cooked pasta to the pan or combine everything in an ovenproof dish. Mix the pasta and sauce together until nearly combined, adding a little of the reserved water, if necessary, to loosen the sauce. Tear in the mozzarella and basil, then mix everything together well. Scatter sover the crumb topping, if using.

Bake in the preheated oven for 25–35 minutes until the crumb topping is lovely and golden.

Cook's note I usually prepare and cook my pasta bakes in a large ovenproof saucepan, so I only need to use one pan. If you don't have this sort of pan, use your usual saucepan for preparing the pasta and then bake it all in an ovenproof dish.

One-Pot Tomato and Mascarpone Pasta

What I love about a one-pot pasta dish is that the starch from the pasta helps to make a lovely, glossy sauce as it cooks. It's even better when that sauce is the classic flavour combination of tomato and mascarpone. I squeeze on a bit of lemon juice at the end to elevate it that little bit more.

SERVES 4–6

1 tablespoon olive oil
1 onion, finely chopped
1 red (bell) pepper, chopped
2 garlic cloves, crushed or finely grated (shredded)
1 teaspoon paprika
1 × 400-g (14-oz) tin chopped tomatoes
3 tablespoons tomato paste (concentrated purée)
500g (1lb 2oz) dried penne
100g (3½oz) mascarpone
Salt and freshly ground black pepper

TO SERVE

1 lemon, zested (optional) and cut into wedges

Heat the oil in a large pan with a lid over a medium heat. Add the onion and red pepper and fry for 5 minutes before adding in the garlic and paprika and frying for 1 minute.

Stir in the tinned tomatoes and tomato paste. Tip in the pasta and pour over 900ml (30fl oz) water. Season really well with salt and freshly ground black pepper and stir. Pop on the lid, then simmer for 10 minutes. Remove the lid, stir to mix everything together then cook for a further 5 minutes.

Stir in the mascarpone and lemon zest. Serve with the lemon wedges, if you like.

Halloumi and Ratatouille Traybake

One-pot, one-tin and traybake recipes have taken the cookery world by storm. It's no surprise because they're easy to throw together and generate less washing up. The perfect one-pot requires no side dishes but includes every element of a main meal. This is why tinned tomatoes are an ideal traybake ingredient; with a quick pour and stir, there's no need for an additional sauce. This traybake includes potatoes, so your carbohydrate quota is sorted and is great on its own, but I like to serve it with couscous or crusty bread as well.

SERVES 4

350g (12½oz) baby potatoes, cut into bite-sized chunks
3 tablespoons olive oil
2 courgettes (zucchini), chopped
2 red onions, peeled and cut into 8 wedges
1 red (bell) pepper, chopped into bite-sized pieces
A few thyme sprigs
1 × 400-g (14-oz) tin chopped tomatoes
Handful of torn basil leaves
250g (9oz) halloumi, cut into 8 slices
Salt and freshly ground black pepper

Preheat the oven to 200°C/180°C fan/390°F/gas 6.

Tip the potato chunks into a large roasting tin (sheet pan) and drizzle over 1 tablespoon oil. Season with salt and freshly ground black pepper and toss to coat the potatoes. Roast in the hot oven for 10 minutes or until beginning to soften.

Remove the tin from the oven. Tip in the courgette, red onion, red pepper and thyme, then drizzle in 1½ tablespoons oil and toss everything together. Return the tin to the oven and roast for a further 20–25 minutes or until the potatoes are tender and all the veg is a little charred.

Pour over the tinned tomatoes and mix everything together. Lay the halloumi slices over the top of the veg, brush each slice with a little oil and season them well. Cook for around 15 minutes or until golden.

Scatter over the torn basil leaves just before serving.

Make it meaty Put 6 sausages into the roasting tin (sheet pan) at the same time as the potatoes and continue to cook the dish as instructed above.

Chickpea, Cavolo Nero and Harissa Stew

Tinned tomatoes are great for making a rich sauce, whether as the main attraction or a support act for other headline ingredients; here they're the perfect base for loading with veg and spicing up with harissa. I often make a spin on this dish, including whatever veg I've got lying around and swapping new potatoes for sweet potatoes, cavolo nero for spinach or cabbage and courgette (zucchini) for a red (bell) pepper.

SERVES 4

2 tablespoons olive oil
1 onion, sliced
2 garlic cloves, crushed or finely chopped
1 courgette (zucchini), chopped
350g (12½oz) baby potatoes, chopped into bite-sized pieces
1–2 tablespoons rose harissa paste
1 × 400-g (14-oz) tin chickpeas (garbanzo beans), drained
1 × 400-g (14-oz) tin chopped tomatoes, plum tomatoes or cherry tomatoes
500ml (17fl oz) vegetable stock
150g (5½oz) cavolo nero, tough stalks removed and leaves chopped
Salt and freshly ground black pepper

TO SERVE
Parmesan cheese or vegetarian or vegan Italian hard cheese, grated (shredded)
Plain couscous or thick slices of crusty bread (optional)

Heat the oil in a large saucepan with a lid over a medium heat. Add the onion and fry for 8–10 minutes or until beginning to brown.

Tip in the garlic and cook for 1 minute before stirring in the courgette and cooking for around 5 minutes or until starting to soften.

Tumble in the potatoes, stir through the harissa and cook for 5–8 minutes or until the potatoes are beginning to colour.

Scatter in the chickpeas and pour in the tinned tomatoes and stock. Season well with salt and freshly ground black pepper and stir everything together, pop on the lid and simmer for 15–20 minutes or until the potatoes are tender. Check the liquid levels: the sauce should have thickened a little, but you still want plenty of juices. So, if it's getting slightly dry, pour in a splash of hot water.

Once the potatoes are tender, stir in the cavolo nero and simmer for 3 minutes.

Serve with a scattering of Parmesan. This dish goes well with some couscous or slices of crusty bread, if you prefer.

Spinach and Tomato Strata

Sometimes known as a breakfast casserole, a strata is a great brunch dish. If ever I'm too late to the shop to pick up a fresh baguette, I buy a couple of bake-at-home ones and cook them as soon as I get home to give them enough time to cool down before making this dish. Strata goes really well with a couple of sausages on the side and it's also fab with my Tomato Ketchup (page 148).

SERVES 4–6

50g (1¾ oz) butter, softened, plus extra
    for greasing
1 large baguette, sliced into 3-cm (1-inch)
    thick slices
1 × 400-g (14-oz) tin chopped tomatoes
150g (5½oz) frozen spinach
    (around 4 blocks), defrosted
6 eggs, beaten
100ml (3½fl oz) milk
1 tablespoon dried mixed herbs
100g (3½oz) Cheddar cheese, grated
    (shredded)
Salt and freshly ground black pepper

Preheat the oven to 180°C/160°C fan/350°F/gas 4. Grease a medium-sized ovenproof baking dish with butter.

Butter one side of each baguette slice. Arrange the bread in the baking dish so that one long side of the crust is touching the base of the dish.

In a jug (pitcher) or bowl, combine the tinned tomatoes, spinach, eggs, milk, herbs, half the cheese and a good seasoning of salt and freshly ground black pepper. Pour this mixture over the bread slices, ensuring the spinach is evenly distributed over the slices. You can also tuck some spinach in between the bread, if you like.

Scatter the remaining cheese over the top and bake in the hot oven for 35–45 minutes or until the cheese is golden and the bread has puffed up.

Sweet Potato, Butter Bean and Peanut Stew

This stew is a household favourite. It's hearty and comforting, but with flavours that feel super fresh. It's also surprisingly quick to make. The peanuts, coriander (cilantro) and lime to serve are important, so I strongly recommend not leaving them out. The crunch of the peanut and the zing of the lime really bring the dish to life.

SERVES 4–6

1 tablespoon sunflower or vegetable oil
1 onion, chopped
1 red (bell) pepper, chopped
Thumb-sized piece of fresh root ginger, finely grated (shredded)
4 garlic cloves, chopped or crushed
1–2 teaspoons chilli powder (depending on how hot you like it)
2 sweet potatoes, peeled and roughly chopped
1 × 400-g (14-oz) tin chopped tomatoes or plum tomatoes
2 tablespoons tomato paste (concentrated purée)
75g (2½oz) crunchy peanut butter
1 × 400-g (14-oz) tin coconut milk
250ml (9fl oz) vegetable stock
1 × 400-g (14-oz) tin butter beans (lima beans), drained and rinsed

TO SERVE
Handful of torn coriander (cilantro) leaves
Handful of roughly chopped unsalted peanuts
1–2 limes, cut into wedges

Heat the oil in a large saucepan with a lid over a medium-low heat. Add the onion and red pepper and fry for 8–10 minutes or until softened and beginning to brown. Stir in the ginger and garlic and cook for a further 1 minute.

Stir in the chilli powder, then tip in the sweet potatoes and mix everything together. Cook for a few minutes to soften the potatoes then tip in the tinned tomatoes, tomato paste and peanut butter and stir well.

Pour in the coconut milk and stock. Bring to the boil, then turn down the heat, cover and simmer for 10 minutes before tipping in the butter beans and cooking with the lid off for 20–25 minutes or until the potatoes and beans are tender and the sauce has thickened slightly.

Serve with a scattering of chopped coriander and peanuts plus lime wedges to squeeze over.

Tomato and Red Pepper Soup with Pesto

It's always useful to have a quick soup recipe up your sleeve, whether it's for a quick lunch or a dinner-party starter. This one is super speedy can be made even simpler by using roasted red (bell) peppers from a jar. I've topped this soup with a pesto, which just makes the whole thing pop with a lovely flavour boost.

SERVES 2 AS A MAIN OR 4 AS A STARTER

2 red (bell) peppers or 2 roasted red (bell) peppers from a jar
2 tablespoons olive oil
1 onion, chopped
2 garlic cloves, crushed or chopped
1 teaspoon dried mixed herbs
1 teaspoon smoked paprika
1 × 400-g (14-oz) tin chopped tomatoes or plum tomatoes
1 vegetable stock cube
50g (1¾oz) pesto, to serve

Blister the red peppers over the flame of a gas hob (stovetop). Alternatively, cut the peppers in half and grill them skin side up under a hot grill (broiler). Once the peppers are completely blackened, pop them inside a reusable sandwich bag or into a bowl and cover with a wax wrap or silicon cover (I try to avoid using clingfilm/plastic wrap whenever possible). When the peppers are cool enough to handle, peel the blackened skins off, discard the skins and chop the roasted flesh into pieces. Set the roasted peppers to one side.

Heat the oil in a saucepan with a lid over a gentle heat. Add the onion and fry for 8–10 minutes or until softened. Stir in the garlic, turn the heat up to medium and cook for 1 minute.

Stir in the herbs and paprika. Tip in the roasted peppers and tinned tomatoes, plus 1½ tins water and the stock cube. Pop on the lid and simmer for 20 minutes.

Blitz the soup in a blender or using a handheld stick (immersion) blender until smooth. Divide the soup between bowls and swirl in a spoonful of pesto to each bowl.

Storage Once blended, you can store this soup in the fridge for a few days or keep it in the freezer for up to 3 months. When ready to serve, defrost the soup and then reheat it until piping hot throughout. Swirl in the pesto just before serving.

Tomato and Butternut Squash Soup

This soup is an easy win for lunch or dinner, but it can also be jazzed up a little with some funky toppings if you want to serve it at a dinner party. The glorious orange colour and sweetness of the squash are just two of its assets, but the tomatoes tone everything down just a little to give the soup a deeper colour and a more grown-up flavour.

SERVES 4–6

2 teaspoons sunflower or vegetable oil
1 onion, chopped
1 garlic clove, crushed or chopped
1 teaspoon ground cumin
1 butternut squash, peeled, de-seeded and chopped
A few thyme sprigs and/or rosemary sprigs or 1 teaspoon dried mixed herbs
1 × 400-g (14-oz) tin chopped tomatoes or plum tomatoes
1 litre (34fl oz) vegetable stock
1 teaspoon Tabasco or to taste
Salt and freshly ground black pepper

Heat the oil in a saucepan with a lid over a medium heat. Add the onion and fry for 6–8 minutes or until soft and beginning to brown. Stir in the garlic, cook for 1 minute then stir in the cumin and cook for 30 seconds.

Tip in the butternut squash pieces and stir to coat them in the spices, cook for a few minutes until starting to soften, then add the herbs, tomatoes, stock and a good seasoning of salt and freshly ground black pepper. Stir, bring to the simmer, pop on the lid and leave to simmer for 30–40 minutes or until the squash is tender.

Blitz the soup in a blender or using a handheld stick (immersion) blender until smooth, then stir through the Tabasco, to taste. Check the seasoning and add more salt and pepper, if necessary, before serving.

Top toppings A drizzle of good-quality olive oil and a scattering of salted roasted pumpkin seeds (pepitas) or squash seeds (as above) add a little sophistication to this dish, if you're serving it at a dinner party. Fried sage leaves also work well, as does a little dollop of pesto.

Storage Once blended, you can store the soup in the fridge for a few days or keep it in the freezer for up to 3 months. When ready to serve, defrost the soup and then reheat it until piping hot throughout.

Family Feasts

Chicken and Chorizo Pie

The pairing of chicken and chorizo never fails to appeal, whether combined
in a paella, tossed through pasta or, like here, served in a pie. The smokiness
of the chorizo, enhanced by the paprika, goes really well with tomatoes.
As with pretty much every pie I've ever eaten, this one is great served
with buttery mash and steamed greens.

SERVES 6–8

1 tablespoon olive oil
6 boneless, skinless chicken thighs,
    chopped into bite-sized pieces
1 onion, finely chopped
1 carrot, finely chopped
1 celery stick, finely chopped
200g (7oz) cooking chorizo, chopped
2 garlic cloves, crushed or chopped
2 teaspoons smoked paprika
3 thyme sprigs or 2 teaspoons dried
    mixed herbs
1 × 400-g (14-oz) tin chopped tomatoes
200ml (7fl oz) chicken stock
1 × 320-g (11-oz) packet ready-rolled
    puff pastry
1 egg, beaten, to glaze
Salt and freshly ground black pepper

Heat ½ tablespoon oil in a frying pan (skillet) or saucepan
over medium heat. Add the chicken and cook until golden
all over, about 4 minutes. Transfer the chicken from the pan
to a plate, leaving the oil behind, and set aside.

Drizzle the remaining oil into the pan and add the onion,
carrot and celery. Cook over a gentle heat for 10–12 minutes
until soft but not golden. Stir in the cooking chorizo, turn up
the heat a little and fry for a few minutes before adding the
garlic, smoked paprika, thyme or mixed herbs and a good
seasoning of salt and pepper. Fry for 1 minute then tip in the
cooked chicken, tinned tomatoes and chicken stock. Cook
for 15 minutes to thicken up the sauce a little and then
remove the pan from the heat.

Preheat the oven to 200°C/180°C fan/390°F/gas 6.

Tip the chicken and chorizo filling into an ovenproof pie dish.
Unroll the puff pastry sheet and lay it over the top of the pie
filling. Remove any excess pastry from around the lip of
the pie dish and crimp the edge, pressing down on the rim
of the dish to seal. You can decorate the pie top using any of
the excess pastry scraps, if you like. Brush the pastry all over
with the beaten egg, then pierce the pie top with a couple of
holes to let the steam escape. Bake in the preheated oven
for 30–40 minutes until the pastry is golden.

Prep ahead This pie will keep in the fridge, covered, for a
couple of days, if you want to make it ahead of time. For best
results, I prefer to make and store only the pie filling and
then add the pastry top to the pie and glaze it just before
baking. Alternatively, make the full pie, cover it, then freeze
uncooked. Cook from frozen for 45 minutes–1 hour.

Garlic and Tomato Roast Chicken

My Grandad introduced me to the joys of slathering a chicken in garlic. I don't just mean a few cloves, I mean a few heads of garlic. I tone it down a little nowadays, but I still include his overnight marinating technique, so you do need to plan ahead. The tomatoes as the base impart the chicken with flavour throughout the cooking process and they give you an instant sauce at the end.

SERVES 6

1 head garlic or 12 cloves (you can use less for a milder garlic flavour)
6 tablespoons olive oil
1 whole chicken (around 1.5kg/3 lb 5oz)
1 × 400-g (14-oz) tin chopped tomatoes or plum tomatoes
2 carrots, roughly chopped
2 celery sticks, roughly chopped
1 onion, roughly chopped
1 tablespoon dried mixed herbs
1 chicken stock cube or 200ml (7fl oz) chicken stock (gluten-free, if necessary)
Freshly ground black pepper

Peel 8 garlic cloves. Crush the peeled cloves with the oil. Loosen the skin around the chicken breast, then spread the garlic paste under the skin. Place the chicken upside down in a roasting tin (sheet pan) and leave overnight in the fridge. (You can skip this, but it infuses the meat with garlic flavour.)

The next day, turn over the chicken and place it in the roasting tray breast side up. Brush any oil that escaped the chicken over the skin and season the meat all over.

Preheat the oven to 220°C/200°C/430°F/gas 7.

Roast the chicken in the hot oven for 20 minutes, then turn the heat down to 180°C/160°C fan/350°F/gas 4.

Remove the tin from the oven and pour the tinned tomatoes around the chicken. Scatter in the veg along with the remaining garlic cloves and herbs. Combine the stock cube with 200ml (7fl oz) water and pour over the chicken. Season well with pepper (the stock cube will likely be salty enough) and mix everything up. Return the tin to the oven and cook for 1 hour–1 hour 30 minutes or until the chicken is cooked through, its juices run clear or its internal temperature at the thickest point is 70°C/160°F on a probe thermometer.

Leave the chicken to rest while you tend to the sauce. Pull out the garlic cloves and carefully squeeze the cooked garlic from the skins – you need to make sure they're cool enough or use gloves so you don't burn yourself. Mix the garlic through the tomatoes. You now have a few options: you can leave the sauce as it is and have a chunky sauce; you can strain the sauce through a sieve (strainer) into a bowl or jug (pitcher), discard the cooked veg and use the liquid as a thin sauce; or you can blend some of the veg with the liquid to give you a thicker sauce; or you can use the liquid as the base of your gravy. Whichever you choose, it'll be delicious.

Carve the roast chicken into slices and serve with the sauce.

Chicken Milanese

Crispy breaded chicken escalopes are famous all over the world. Whether as Milanese or schnitzel, or even with the chicken swapped out for veal. Pairing it with pasta in a tomato sauce is not a new invention, but simply my favourite way to eat Chicken Milanese, especially with a good squeeze of lemon juice.

SERVES 2

FOR THE SAUCE
1 teaspoon olive oil
½ red onion, finely chopped
1 garlic clove, finely grated (shredded)
1 × 227-g (8-oz) tin chopped tomatoes
1 teaspoon tomato paste
  (concentrated purée)
Pinch of sugar
¼ teaspoon red wine vinegar

FOR THE CHICKEN
2 chicken breasts
2 tablespoons plain (all-purpose) flour
1 egg, beaten
75g (2½oz) panko breadcrumbs
20g (¾oz) Parmesan cheese, finely
  grated (shredded)
2 tablespoons olive oil
Salt and freshly ground black pepper

TO SERVE
200g (7oz) dried spaghetti
Handful of torn basil leaves
1 lemon, cut into wedges

Cook's tip If, like me, you use the same frying pan (skillet) for the sauce and chicken, you can reheat the sauce with the spaghetti in the saucepan it was boiled in after you've drained the spaghetti.

First, make the sauce. Heat the oil in a frying pan (skillet) over a gentle heat. Add the onion and fry for 6–8 minutes or until softened. Stir in the garlic and fry for 1 minute before tipping in the tinned tomatoes, tomato paste, sugar and vinegar. Mix to combine and simmer gently for 5–10 minutes to thicken slightly. Turn off the heat and leave while you make the chicken escalopes.

Place the chicken breasts between two pieces of parchment paper and bash with a rolling pin to flatten them out to half their thickness. Tip the flour onto a plate and season with salt and freshly ground black pepper. Mix to combine and set aside. Pour the beaten egg onto another plate and set aside. Combine the panko with the Parmesan on a third plate and set aside.

First, put one of the chicken breasts onto the plate of flour and ensure it's fully coated on both sides. Next, dip the chicken in the beaten egg and, finally, in the breadcrumbs, again ensuring it's completely covered. Repeat with the second chicken breast.

Bring a pan of salted water to the boil and cook the spaghetti according to the packet instructions; this should take around 10 minutes.

Meanwhile, heat 2 tablespoons oil in a large frying pan over a medium heat. Add the breaded chicken and cook for around 4 minutes on each side or until golden and cooked through.

Drain the spaghetti, reserving a little of the pasta cooking water. Reheat the sauce and combine it with the spaghetti, adding a little of the reserved water, if necessary, to loosen the sauce. Pile the spaghetti onto plates and top with the breadcrumbed chicken.

Scatter over a few basil leaves, then serve with the lemon wedges for squeezing over.

Chicken Cacciatore

In Italian, 'cacciatore' means hunter. This refers to the meal being hunter-style as it was typically made with ingredients that were locally hunted or foraged. The cacciatore would also usually be made with plum tomatoes instead of chopped tomatoes but I prefer the texture of the chopped tomatoes, although mixing it up with plum tomatoes is a nice option. This is great served with crusty bread or orzo.

SERVES 4–6

3 tablespoons olive oil
6 bone-in, skin-on chicken thighs
250g (9 oz) chestnut mushrooms, sliced
1 onion, sliced
1 red (bell) pepper, chopped
1 carrot, chopped
2 garlic cloves, crushed or finely chopped
125ml (4fl oz) white wine
2 × 400-g (14-oz) tins chopped or plum
  tomatoes
100ml (3½fl oz) chicken stock
  (gluten-free, if necessary)
4 tablespoons tomato paste
  (concentrated purée)
2 rosemary sprigs
2 thyme sprigs
2 bay leaves
75g (2½oz) pitted black olives
Salt and freshly ground black pepper

Heat 1 tablespoon oil in a large, non-stick frying pan (skillet) with a lid and brown the chicken for a few minutes until golden all over (it doesn't need to be cooked through). Remove from the pan and set aside.

Fry the mushrooms in the same pan until they've released their liquid and browned. This can take several minutes. Remove from the pan and set aside.

Drizzle the remaining oil into the pan and, over a low heat, fry the onion, red pepper and carrot until beginning to soften but not golden. Stir in the garlic and cook for 1 minute. Pour in the wine, cook for a couple of minutes to cook off the alcohol then add the tinned tomatoes, chicken stock, tomato paste and herbs. Return the previously cooked chicken and mushrooms to the pan. Season well, cover the pan with the lid and simmer gently, over a low heat, for 45 minutes.

After 45 minutes, remove the lid, scatter in the olives and simmer, with the lid off, for 10–15 minutes to thicken the sauce a little. If it begins to dry out, add a dash of water. Remove the rosemary and thyme sprigs before serving.

Dad's Healthier Butter Chicken

My Dad has been a curry fan for a long time, since he cooked his way through *Pat Chapman's Curry Bible*. He's made some amazing curries over the years, serving up entire feasts on special occasions or just a Friday-night curry whenever the craving hits. This butter chicken curry is his signature dish. Recently, Dad started a blog – dadcookshealthy.com – to share his favourite recipes that he's adapted to make healthier. This was his very first post.

SERVES 4

4 chicken breasts, cut into bite-sized chunks
juice of 1 lime

FOR THE MARINADE

50g (1¾oz) natural yogurt
50g (1¾oz) single (pure) cream
2 garlic cloves, crushed or finely grated (shredded)
25g (¾oz) fresh root ginger, crushed or finely grated
1 teaspoon garam masala
1 teaspoon ground turmeric
1 teaspoon ground cumin

FOR THE SAUCE

1 teaspoon sunflower or vegetable oil
3 garlic cloves, finely grated (shredded)
25g (¾oz) fresh root ginger, finely grated (shredded)
1 × 400-g (14-oz) tin chopped tomatoes
1 teaspoon ground coriander
1 teaspoon ground cumin
½ teaspoon ground cinnamon
1 teaspoon garam masala
1 teaspoon desiccated coconut
15g (½oz) cashew nuts
15g (½oz) pumpkin seeds (pepitas)
1 teaspoon salt
200ml (7fl oz) boiling water

Mix the chicken breast pieces with the lime juice. Place in the fridge and leave for 1 hour.

Combine all the ingredients for the marinade in a bowl. Take the chicken from the fridge and drain off the lime juice. Stir the chicken pieces into the marinade and leave for at least 4 hours or overnight.

Once the chicken has finished marinating, preheat the oven to 220°C/200°C fan/430°F/gas 7.

Take the chicken pieces out of the marinade, shaking them to remove any excess (but keeping the marinade for later). Thread the chicken onto skewers leaving a space between each piece. Suspend the chicken skewers over a roasting tin (sheet pan). Alternatively, put the chicken pieces into a non-stick roasting tin. Cook in the hot oven for 15–20 minutes.

While the chicken is cooking, make the sauce. Heat the oil in a non-stick saucepan with a lid over a medium heat. Add the garlic and ginger and cook, stirring continuously, for 1 minute. Stir in the tinned tomatoes and bring to a simmer, then mix in all the spices, coconut and 1 teaspoon salt.

Blend the cashews and pumpkin seeds with the boiling water in a food processor or using a handheld stick (immersion) blender. Stir this mixture into the tomato sauce.

Stir the cooked chicken and reserved marinade into the sauce, put the lid on the pan and simmer for 10 minutes or until the chicken is cooked through.

Weeknight curry For an even quicker version, try the Makhani Sauce on page 154.

Chicken and Harissa Traybake with Tahini Drizzle

Although this is a traybake, it's much jazzier than most and definitely straddles the border of a midweek meal and a fancy feast. It can, if you're a reasonably quick cook, take under an hour to bring together. The tinned tomatoes, here, are the saviour that swoops in at the end to make it all come together. Try serving with couscous or a fresh green salad.

SERVES 4–6

2 tablespoons harissa (use a little less if yours is particularly spicy)
3 tablespoons olive oil
Zest and juice of 1 lime
1kg (21b 4oz) bone-in, skin-on chicken thighs (around 6–8)
600g (1lb 5oz) sweet potatoes, peeled and chopped into bite-sized pieces
2 red onions, peeled and cut into 8 wedges
1 × 400-g (14-oz) tin chickpeas (garbanzo beans), drained
1 × 400-g (14-oz) tin chopped tomatoes
Salt and freshly ground black pepper

FOR THE TAHINI DRIZZLE
40g (1½oz) tahini
150ml (5½fl oz) natural yogurt

Preheat the oven to 200°C/180°C fan/390°F/gas 6.

Combine the harissa, 1 tablespoon oil and lime zest in a small bowl. Season with salt and freshly ground black pepper. Tip the chicken thighs into a bowl and drizzle over the harissa mixture. Using your hands (wearing gloves, if you need to), mix everything together so that the chicken is fully coated. Set aside.

Tip the sweet potato pieces and red onion wedges into a large roasting tin (sheet pan), drizzle over 2 tablespoons oil, season well with salt and freshly ground black pepper and toss everything together. Lay the chicken on top of the vegetables and roast in the hot oven for 20 minutes.

Remove the tray from the oven and scatter around the chickpeas. Give everything a shake and return to the oven. Turn up the oven temperature to 220°C/200°C fan/430°F/gas 7 and roast for a further 15 minutes. Remove the tray from the oven again and pour the tinned tomatoes around the chicken pieces. Mix a little with a spoon and return to the oven for a final 10 minutes.

Combine the tahini and yogurt with the juice of ½–1 lime, to taste. (I love lime, so I add all the juice, but you might like a little less.) Season, mix again and add a splash of water, if needed – it should be thick but also possible to drizzle.

Remove the chicken traybake from the oven and drizzle over the tahini sauce before serving.

Lamb and Spinach Curry

I love spinach in a curry and this one is spiced similarly to a bhuna.
If you prefer, you can use chicken thighs or beef and it will taste just
as delicious. Serve with your favourite curry accompaniments.

SERVES 4

2 tablespoons sunflower or vegetable oil
2 onions, sliced
400g (14oz) diced lamb leg or shoulder
4 garlic cloves, crushed or finely grated
  (shredded)
Thumb-sized piece of fresh root ginger,
  peeled and finely grated (shredded)
½ small bunch of coriander (cilantro),
  leaves and stalks separated, both
  chopped
1–2 red chillies, finely chopped
2 teaspoons garam masala
1 teaspoon ground cumin
1 teaspoon ground coriander
½ teaspoon ground turmeric
½ teaspoon ground cinnamon
1 tablespoon tomato paste
  (concentrated purée)
1 × 400-g (14-oz) tin chopped tomatoes
100g (3½oz) spinach
75ml (5 tablespoons) natural yogurt

TO SERVE
Plain cooked rice or naan bread
Your choice of chutneys

Heat the oil in a large frying pan (skillet) or saucepan. Fry the onion for 6–8 minutes until softened and starting to brown. Stir in the lamb pieces and fry for 5 minutes until browned. Tip in the garlic, ginger and coriander stalks and cook for 2 minutes, stirring well to combine everything.

Stir in the chillies and spices and cook for 2 minutes being careful not to burn them. If they start to stick or burn, add a splash of water. Squeeze in the tomato paste, stir to mix everything together and then pour in the tinned tomatoes. Half fill the tin with water and add that too. Simmer for around 15 minutes until the sauce has thickened nicely and the meat is tender.

Tip in the spinach, mix in and cook for 2 minutes until wilted. Spoon in the yogurt and cook for 1 minute before serving.

Serve the curry with plain rice or naan bread and any chutneys on the side.

Lasagne

Pasta, tomatoes, cheese, great with garlic bread; I'll be having seconds, thank you. When I make this lasagne, I usually use half a batch of the ragù on page 45. I've included instructions here for a quicker ragù, which I use when I don't have any of my usual ragù in the freezer. It's delicious and makes it all a little quicker when cooking from scratch. I put a layer of pasta down first because it makes it easier to scoop the lasagne out of the dish without losing structural integrity.

SERVES 6

12–16 lasagne sheets
40g (1½oz) Parmesan cheese, grated (shredded)
¼ whole nutmeg

FOR THE RAGÙ

1 tablespoon olive oil
1 carrot, finely diced
1 onion, finely diced
1 celery stick, finely diced
2 garlic cloves, crushed or finely grated (shredded)
400–500g (14oz–1lb 2oz) minced (ground) beef
2 thyme sprigs
2 rosemary sprigs
1 bay leaf
125ml (4½fl oz) red wine
1 × 400-g (14-oz) tin chopped tomatoes
1 tablespoon tomato paste (concentrated purée)
125ml (4½fl oz) beef stock
Salt and freshly ground black pepper

FOR THE BÉCHAMEL SAUCE

850ml (29fl oz) milk
½ onion
2 bay leaves
75g (2½oz) butter
75g (2½oz) plain (all-purpose) flour

First, make the ragù. Heat the oil in a very large saucepan over a gentle heat. Tip in the carrot, onion and celery, put the lid on and cook for 15 minutes, stirring occasionally, until softened but not golden.

Stir in the garlic and cook for a further 1 minute before tipping in the beef. Break up the meat with a wooden spoon and fry until browned.

Stir in the herbs and red wine, simmer for a few minutes, then tip in the tinned tomatoes, tomato paste and beef stock. Season well with salt and freshly ground black pepper. Simmer for 30 minutes, stirring occasionally. If after this time the sauce needs to thicken a little more, cook it for a further 10–15 minutes. Set aside.

Next, make the béchamel sauce. Heat the milk in a small pan with the onion, bay leaves and a good pinch of salt and pepper. Remove from the heat once simmering.

Melt the butter in a small pan over a low heat. Once melted, stir the flour into the butter until a thick paste has formed. Ladle in the warm milk, one ladleful at a time, and whisk continuously until each ladleful has been absorbed. Continue until all the milk has been used up and you have a silky sauce. Simmer for 1 minute and set aside.

Preheat the oven to 200°C/180°C fan/390°F/gas 6.

Cover the base of an ovenproof dish with a layer of lasagne sheets. Spoon half the ragù into the dish and follow this with a further layer of lasagne sheets, then cover with half the béchamel. Add the rest of the ragù, then another layer of lasagne sheets and end with the remaining béchamel. Finally, scatter over the Parmesan and grate over the nutmeg.

Cook in the hot oven for 35–45 minutes or until the lasagne is cooked through, the pasta sheets are tender and the cheese top is golden.

Slow-Braised Beef and Rosemary One-Pot

Although lamb is most often paired with rosemary, I find that beef works just as well, plus the cost is much more manageable. Another benefit is that beef and tomatoes are a match made in heaven. This is perfect for when you want a roast that requires minimal effort for maximum flavour. Any leftovers are great during the following week served with some fresh mash and/or steamed veg for a quick evening meal.

SERVES 6–8

1kg (2lb 4oz) beef braising joint (such as brisket or chuck)
3 tablespoons olive oil
8 shallots, peeled and quartered
4 carrots, chopped
6–8 rosemary sprigs
300ml (10fl oz) beef stock
200ml (7fl oz) red wine
2 tablespoons tomato paste (concentrated purée)
2 × 400-g (14-oz) tins chopped tomatoes, plum tomatoes, cherry tomatoes or tomato passata (puréed tomatoes)
Salt and freshly ground black pepper

Pat the beef dry with kitchen paper and season well with salt and freshly ground black pepper. Heat 1 tablespoon oil in a large, heavy-based saucepan with a lid over a medium heat. Brown the beef all over, this may take a good 5–10 minutes. Remove the beef from the pan, leaving any oil behind in the pan, and set aside.

While the beef is cooling, heat the remaining oil in the same pan on a medium-low heat. Add the shallots and carrots and fry for around 5 minutes or until they begin to soften and take on a bit of colour. Turn off the heat.

Using a sharp knife, make around 8–10 slits in the flesh of the beef. Snap off bits from the rosemary sprigs and tuck them into the cuts. Put the beef into the pan with the shallots and carrots, then add the remaining rosemary, stock, wine, tomato paste and tinned tomatoes. Season well with salt and freshly ground black pepper.

Bring the sauce to a simmer, pop the lid on the pan and cook gently for 4 hours or until the beef is tender and the sauce has thickened. Check a few times during cooking and give it a stir.

Slow cooking After browning the beef and frying the shallots and carrots in a pan, you can then move everything to a slow cooker and cook on high for 7 hours. This recipe can also be slow roasted in the oven. Cook at 170°C/150°C fan/340°F/gas 3½ for 6 hours or until the beef is tender.

Goulash

Goulash originated in Hungary, but went on to grow in popularity all over central Europe. This paprika-heavy version began much later, but makes sense to me because paprika, tomatoes and beef are a great combination. Slow-cooking the beef in the tomatoes makes the meat incredibly tender and the sauce rich and flavourful. It's great served with boiled potatoes or plain rice.

SERVES 4-6

2 tablespoons sunflower or vegetable oil
600g (1lb 5oz) stewing or braising steak
2 onions, sliced
1 red (bell) pepper, chopped
1 green (bell) pepper, chopped
2 garlic cloves, crushed or finely chopped
1 tablespoon hot smoked paprika
2 tablespoons paprika
750ml (25fl oz) beef stock
1 × 400-g (14-oz) tin chopped tomatoes
 or plum tomatoes
2 tablespoons tomato paste
 (concentrated purée)
2 bay leaves
2 tablespoons soft light brown sugar
 or granulated white sugar
150ml (5½fl oz) sour cream

TO SERVE
Plain cooked rice or boiled potatoes

Preheat the oven to 180°C/160°C fan/350°F/gas 4.

Heat 1 tablespoon oil in a large ovenproof pan with a lid over a medium heat. Add the beef and brown it all over – you may need to do this in batches. Remove the beef from the pan, leaving the oil behind, and set aside.

Tip the onions into the same pan and fry for 8–10 minutes or until softened and beginning to brown. Stir in the red and green peppers and cook for 5 minutes to soften before mixing in the garlic and cooking for 1 minute.

Sprinkle in both paprikas and mix to coat everything, then pour in the stock and tinned tomatoes, squeeze in the tomato paste and stir in the bay leaves and sugar.

Return the beef to the pan, bring to a simmer, pop on the lid and place in the oven for 1 hour 30 minutes–2 hours or until the beef is melt-in-the-mouth tender.

Remove from the oven and stir through the sour cream before serving.

Serve with plain rice or boiled potatoes.

Storage You can store this goulash in the fridge for a few days or keep it in the freezer for up to 3 months. If freezing, do not add the cream before storing. When ready to serve, defrost the goulash if frozen, then reheat it until piping hot throughout. It should reach 70°C/160°F on a probe thermometer. Stir through the cream before serving.

Paccheri Pasta Pie

While you may look at this recipe and think 'simple pasta bake', it's a much more involved version. If you're looking for a crowd-pleasing meal that's suitable for a fancier occasion than a regular midweek dinner, this a great option. It combines all the family friendly flavours: sausage, tomato and cheese being the big three. If you can't find paccheri – very large pasta tubes – then you can, of course, serve this as a pasta bake; it's equally delicious.

SERVES 6

1 tablespoon olive oil
1 red onion, chopped
1 carrot, grated (shredded) or finely chopped
2 garlic cloves, crushed or finely grated (shredded)
6 pork sausages
8 sage leaves, finely chopped
A few thyme sprigs
150ml (5½fl oz) red wine
1 × 400-g (14-oz) tin chopped tomatoes
1 tablespoon tomato paste (concentrated purée)
500g (1lb 2oz) paccheri pasta (or large rigatoni or any other large pasta tube will work)
50g (1¾ oz) Parmesan cheese, grated (shredded)
1 × 125-g (4½-oz) mozzarella ball, torn into small pieces

Heat the oil in a large frying pan (skillet) or saucepan over a gentle heat. Add the onion and carrot and fry for 10–12 minutes or until softened. Stir in the garlic and cook for 1 minute.

Squeeze the meat out of the sausage skins directly into the pan. Squashing the sausagemeat down and breaking it up with a wooden spoon, cook for 4–5 minutes until browned.

Stir in the sage and thyme, cook for 30 seconds, then tip in the wine and cook for a couple of minutes until the alcohol has cooked off and the liquid has evaporated a little.

Stir in the tinned tomatoes and tomato paste. Simmer for 5–10 minutes to thicken. Turn off the heat and set aside once done.

Preheat the oven to 200°C/180°C fan/390°F/gas 6.

Meanwhile, bring a large pan of salted water to the boil and cook the paccheri (or other pasta tubes) for around 8 minutes or until almost cooked yet still a little firm. Drain and combine with the sausagemeat sauce.

Arrange the paccheri in an ovenproof dish, placing the pasta tubes so that the open ends face upwards. Pack the tubes into the dish so that they fit snugly. Spoon any leftover sauce into the tubes then scatter over the Parmesan and mozzarella.

Bake in the hot oven for 20–25 minutes until the pasta is completely cooked through and the cheese has melted and become golden.

Enchiladas

Wrapping tortillas around a tasty filling goes back to Aztec times, with recipes for enchiladas appearing hundreds of years ago. These are an anglicised version of the Mexican dish. I prefer enchiladas to fajitas because there's no need to worry about over-stuffing the first wraps and ending up with just a teaspoonful of filling for the final one. With enchiladas, everything is divvied up at the beginning and there's no need to keep one eye on your guests' portion sizes. Especially reassuring for those of us who grew up with greedy siblings!

SERVES 4–8

3 tablespoons oil

2 onions, 1 finely chopped and 1 finely sliced

4 garlic cloves, crushed or finely grated (shredded)

1 red chilli (deseeded if necessary), finely chopped

1 tablespoon smoked paprika

1 teaspoon ground cumin

2 × 400-g (14-oz) tin chopped tomatoes or 1 × 600-g (1lb 5-oz) jar tomato passata (puréed tomatoes)

2 (bell) peppers, any colour, thinly sliced

400g (14oz) chicken breasts, sliced

1 × 400-g (14-oz) tin black beans, pinto beans or red kidney beans, drained and rinsed

8 corn tortillas

100g (3½oz) Cheddar cheese, grated (shredded)

Salt and freshly ground black pepper

TO SERVE

Handful of chopped coriander (cilantro)

150ml (5½fl oz) sour cream

Heat 1 tablespoon oil in a large frying pan (skillet) over a low heat. Add the chopped onion and cook for 8–10 minutes or until softened. Stir in half the garlic and all the red chilli, then cook for 1 minute. Next, stir in 1 teaspoon paprika and the ground cumin and cook for a further 1 minute.

Stir in 1½ tins chopped tomatoes or three-quarters of the tomato passata. Season with salt and pepper. Simmer for 10–15 minutes until reduced. To prevent the tortillas turning soggy during baking, the water must evaporate. Tip the sauce into a bowl or jug (pitcher) and set aside. Wipe out the pan.

Preheat the oven to 200°C/180°C fan/390°F/gas 6.

Heat the remaining oil in the same pan, add the sliced onions and peppers and fry for 10–12 minutes or until softened and any liquid has evaporated. Add the remaining garlic and cook for 1 minute. Stir in the sliced chicken and cook for 5–8 minutes or until browned all over and any liquid that is released has evaporated.

Stir in the paprika and cook for 1 minute. Next, tip in the black beans and remaining tinned tomatoes or passata and cook for 5 minutes or until the chicken is cooked through.

Get an ovenproof baking dish ready (it needs to be big enough to fit 8 rolled-up tortillas and deep enough for the sauce to be poured over). Take a tortilla, fill it with one-eighth of the mixture and roll it up. Tuck the tortilla into the dish; I place these so the seam is facing down to prevent them unrolling. Repeat with the remaining tortillas. Pour the tomato sauce over the tortillas and scatter over the cheese.

Bake in the hot oven for 30–40 minutes or until piping hot and the cheese is golden.

Scatter the coriander over the top and serve at the table with sour cream.

Weeknight Chilli con Carne

When I was at university, I pretty much lived off chilli con carne during the week. That and baked beans on toast. I loved how I could make big batches of chilli and that it was reasonably nutritious. Then, at the weekends, I could be more adventurous depending on what we might have cooked on the course during the week. This is a much simpler – and quicker – version than the option for impressing your friends (page 108), but it still makes use of tinned tomatoes to bring the richness and flavour that goes so well with beef.

SERVES 4

1 tablespoon sunflower or vegetable oil
1 onion, finely chopped
1 carrot, finely chopped
1 celery stick, finely chopped
1 red (bell) pepper, chopped
2 garlic cloves, chopped or crushed
400g (14oz) minced (ground) beef
1–3 teaspoons chilli powder
1 × 400-g (14-oz) tin chopped tomatoes
1 × 400-g (14-oz) tin red kidney beans,
    drained and rinsed
1 tablespoon tomato paste
    (concentrated purée)
1 teaspoon dried oregano
1 beef stock cube (gluten-free,
    if necessary)

TO SERVE
Plain cooked rice or corn tortillas
150ml (5½fl oz) sour cream
Cheddar cheese, grated (shredded)
Pickled jalapeños

Heat the oil in a saucepan or large frying pan (skillet) over a medium-low heat. Fry the onion, carrot and celery for 10–12 minutes or until softened. Tip in the red pepper and cook for a further 5 minutes to soften. Stir in the garlic and cook for 1 minute.

Break in the beef, using the back of a wooden spoon to break it up further, and cook until browned.

Next, add the chilli powder. If you're using hot chilli powder, then 1 teaspoon should do it. For mild, you'll need to add closer to 3 teaspoons.

Add all the remaining ingredients plus 1 tin of water. Simmer for 20–30 minutes or until the sauce has thickened nicely.

Serve with rice or tortillas, sour cream, grated cheese and pickled jalapeños, if you fancy.

Chilli pie One of the ways I like to mix things up a little with chilli is to turn it into a pie. Simply pour your chilli mixture into an ovenproof pie dish and top with mashed potato and grated (shredded) Cheddar cheese. To make the mashed potato, boil 1kg (2lb 4oz) chopped potatoes until tender. Mash the potatoes, combining them with 75ml (2½fl oz) milk and 25g (¾oz) butter. Spread the mash over the pie and scatter the grated (shredded) Cheddar over the top. Bake in the oven at 200°C/180°C fan/390°F/gas 6 for 30 minutes or until the cheese is golden and the pie is piping hot. If you're using leftover chilli, you'll need to cook the pie for a further 10–15 minutes if the chilli has come straight from the fridge.

Chilli for Friends

Slow-cooked chilli using ox cheek is a completely different experience to the chilli con carne using minced (ground) beef (page 107). Neither is necessarily better than the other – they merely serve different purposes. Cooking ox cheek slowly makes it melt in the mouth and the sauce is rich and deep. Likewise, the tomatoes, being slow cooked, give a much different flavour.

SERVES 4

1 tablespoon sunflower or vegetable oil
1 ox cheek (about 400–500g/
   14oz–1lb 2oz), cut into pieces
1 onion, finely chopped
1 carrot, finely chopped
1 celery stick, finely chopped
1 red (bell) pepper, chopped
2 garlic cloves, crushed or finely chopped
1½ teaspoons hot chilli powder
   (or use mild if you don't like it too spicy)
2 teaspoons smoked sweet paprika
1 teaspoon ground cumin
2 teaspoons dried oregano
½ teaspoon ground cinnamon
125ml (4fl oz) red wine
1 tablespoon tomato paste
   (concentrated purée)
1 × 400-g (14-oz) tin chopped tomatoes
   or plum tomatoes
1 × 400-g (14-oz) tin red kidney beans,
   drained and rinsed
100g (3½oz) pearl barley (optional)
500ml (18fl oz) beef stock
75g (2½oz) dark (bittersweet) chocolate
   (optional)

TO SERVE
Plain cooked rice or corn tortillas
150ml (5½fl oz) sour cream
Cheddar cheese, grated (shredded)
Pickled jalapeños

Heat the oil in a large saucepan with a lid over a high heat. Add the ox cheek and brown all over. Remove with a slotted spoon, leaving any oil behind, and set aside.

Tip the onion, carrot, celery and red pepper into the same pan, turn down the heat to low and put the lid on. Fry for 10–12 minutes, stirring every few minutes, or until softened but not browned.

Remove the lid and stir in the garlic, fry for 1 minute and then sprinkle in the spices and herbs. Fry for 1 minute, then turn up the heat, pour in the wine and squeeze in the tomato paste. Bring to a simmer, cook for a few minutes and add the tinned tomatoes, red kidney beans, pearl barley, if using, and beef stock. Put the lid back on and simmer on low for 1 hour 30 minutes, stirring every now and then. If the chilli is drying out, add a little water or more stock.

Remove the lid and check the liquid levels (add a few tablespoons water if there's not much liquid left). Give the chilli a good stir, replace the lid and simmer for a further 30 minutes. Check again – if you've used the pearl barley, you may need to add a little water at this point. Put the lid back on and simmer for a final 30 minutes or until the meat is starting to fall apart and the pearl barley is soft. If necessary, simmer for a further 10–20 minutes. Stir through the chocolate, if using, until melted.

Serve with rice or tortillas, sour cream, grated cheese and pickled jalapeños, if you fancy.

Cook's tip If you're sensitive to spice or using a new chilli powder, I recommend adding a little less than usual at first. After 10 minutes of cooking, taste and add more if needed. You can always add more, but you can't take it away!

Three-Bean Chilli

Pulses are a great source of protein and a delicious way to add texture and bulk out a meal. I enjoy the warming qualities this dish offers and when combined with rice and tortilla chips it feels like an indulgent treat. All three chillis on pages 107–109 can be batch cooked, which I recommend. If you're cooking something anyway, you may as well cook more to chuck in the freezer.

SERVES 4

1 tablespoon olive oil
1 onion, finely chopped
1 carrot, finely chopped
1 celery stick, finely chopped
2 (bell) peppers, any colour, chopped
2 garlic cloves, crushed or finely chopped
1 teaspoon dried oregano
1 teaspoon hot chilli powder or
    1 tablespoon mild chilli powder
1 teaspoon smoked paprika
½ teaspoon ground cumin
1 × 400-g (14-oz) tin red kidney beans,
    drained and rinsed
1 × 400-g (14-oz) tin black beans, drained
    and rinsed
1 × 400-g (14-oz) tin borlotti beans
    (cranberry beans), drained and rinsed
1 × 400-g (14-oz) tin chopped tomatoes
2 bay leaves
1½ tablespoons tomato paste
    (concentrated purée)
1 vegetable stock cube (gluten-free,
    if necessary)

TO SERVE

Plain cooked rice or corn tortillas
150ml (5½fl oz) sour cream or plant-
    based alternative
Cheddar cheese or plant-based
    alternative, grated (shredded)
Pickled jalapeños

Heat the oil in a large saucepan with a lid over a gentle heat. Add the onion, carrot and celery and fry with the lid on for 10–12 minutes or until soft but not golden. Tip in the peppers and cook for 5 minutes before stirring in the garlic and cooking for 1 minute. Sprinkle in the dried oregano and spices and give everything a good stir. Cook for 30 seconds.

Tip in the beans. Mix everything round so the beans are coated in the spices then pour in the tinned tomatoes and a tinful of water. Add in the bay leaves, tomato paste and stock cube. Bring to a simmer, pop on the lid and simmer for 15 minutes. Remove the lid and simmer for a further 10–15 minutes or until the sauce has thickened a little and all the veg and beans are tender.

Serve with the usual accompaniments or plant-based alternatives to keep the dish vegan and dairy-free.

Loaded chilli fries For a movie-night treat, try making loaded chilli fries from any leftover chilli. Cook oven fries according to the packet instructions, spoon over any leftover chilli and scatter over 75g (2½oz) grated (shredded) Cheddar and a handful of jalapeños. Bake in the oven at 200°C/180°C fan/390°F/gas 6 for 10–15 minutes or until the cheese has melted and the chilli is warm. Serve with dollops of sour cream and guacamole.

Moroccan-Spiced Vegetable Pie

This is one of my favourite vegetarian dishes and perfect when you want to shove as much of your 5-a-day into one dish. Fellow food writer Felicity Cloake pleaded for lots of veg when she stopped by our place while on a cycling tour. I served her this pie – my vegetarian go-to – and (thankfully) she loved it.

SERVES 4-6

1 butternut squash (approx. 800g/
  1lb 12oz), peeled, deseeded and cut
  into bite-sized pieces
4 banana shallots or 2 red onions, peeled
  and chopped into 8 wedges
3 tablespoons sunflower oil
75g (2½oz) blanched almonds
2 courgettes (zucchini), roughly chopped
3 garlic cloves, chopped or finely grated
  (shredded)
1 teaspoon ground cumin
1 teaspoon ground coriander
1 teaspoon paprika
½ teaspoon ground cinnamon
1 tablespoon tomato paste
  (concentrated purée)
1 × 400-g (14-oz) tin chickpeas
  (garbanzo beans), drained and rinsed
1 × 400-g (14-oz) tin chopped tomatoes
75g (2½oz) raisins
9-12 sheets filo (phyllo) pastry
25g (¾oz) butter, melted
Salt and freshly ground black pepper

Preheat the oven to 200°C/180°C fan/390°F/gas 6.

Tip the squash and shallots or onion pieces into a roasting tin (sheet pan). Drizzle over 2 tablespoons oil, season well with salt and freshly ground black pepper and toss to coat. Roast in the hot oven for 25–30 minutes or until the squash is cooked through and the onion is starting to caramelise.

Toast the almonds in a dry frying pan (skillet) until golden. Remove the almonds from the pan, then add the remaining oil and fry the courgette until turning golden, around 10 minutes. Mix in the garlic and fry for 1 minute, then stir in the spices. Fry for 30 seconds before stirring in the tomato paste, chickpeas, tinned tomatoes, plus a tin of water and the raisins. Cook for 10 minutes to thicken a little, then remove the pan from the heat.

If your frying pan is large enough, mix in the roasted squash, onion and toasted almonds, otherwise combine everything in a bowl. Transfer the mixture to an ovenproof pie dish.

If you haven't already melted the butter, do that now. Unroll the filo pastry. Brush the first filo sheet with a little butter, then loosely scrunch it up and put it on top of the vegetable mixture. Repeat with the remaining sheets, until the vegetables are covered – fewer, looser sheets give a better result than packing it super tight.

Bake in the hot oven for 25–30 minutes until the filo pastry top is golden.

Make it a veggie crumble The base of this pie can also be used for a vegetable crumble. Make a crumble topping by rubbing together 200g (7oz) plain (all-purpose) flour with 100g (3½oz) diced cold butter until you have a breadcrumb texture. Next, mix in 50g (1¾oz) grated (shredded) cheese, such as Cheddar or Gruyère. Season the crumble with plenty of salt and freshly ground black pepper and scatter it over the pie filling. You can also top with some flaked almonds or other chopped nuts.

Stuffed Cabbage Rolls

Cabbage rolls are popular all over the world. In Europe there's a tendency to stuff them with meat, which is what I've done here. Combined with rice and a handful of other flavours, it's almost like a mini meat loaf wrapped in an emerald parcel. They braise gently in the tomatoes while in the oven, which creates an instant sauce. A great option for an alternative Sunday roast.

SERVES 4–6

½ tablespoon olive oil
1 onion, very finely chopped
1 carrot, grated (shredded)
500g (1lb 2oz) minced (ground) beef
1 × 250-g (9-oz) pouch cooked basmati rice
1 teaspoon English mustard (gluten-free, if necessary)
Handful of parsley, finely chopped
125ml (4½fl oz) red wine (optional)
1 × 400-g (14-oz) tin chopped tomatoes
1 tablespoon tomato paste (concentrated purée)
1 teaspoon dried mixed herbs
1 tablespoon red wine vinegar
10–12 cabbage leaves (from 1 large or 2 medium cabbages)
Salt and freshly ground black pepper

Heat the oil in a frying pan (skillet) over a gentle heat. Add the onion and carrot and cook for 10–12 minutes or until softened. Tip into a bowl with the beef, rice, mustard, parsley and a good helping of salt and pepper. Set aside to cool.

Wipe the pan clean and put it back over a medium heat. Pour in the wine and cook for a few minutes to cook off the alcohol. Tip in the tinned tomatoes and squeeze in the tomato paste, then stir in the herbs and vinegar. Season well and simmer for 10–15 minutes to thicken the sauce a little. Set aside while you cook the cabbage leaves.

Peel the leaves from the cabbage until they're slightly smaller than the size of a side plate. You will need around 10–12 leaves. (Don't discard the core of the cabbage as you can use it in soup or serve it as a veg on another day.) Trim any hard stems from the base of the leaves, not all the stem.

Bring a saucepan of salted water to the boil and cook the cabbage leaves for 2–3 minutes to make them easier to handle. Plunge into ice-cold water or rinse under cold running water for a few moments. Pat dry with kitchen paper.

The onion mixture should now be cool enough to handle. Using your hands or a large spoon, combine it all well.

Preheat the oven to 180°C/160°C fan/350°F/gas 4.

Form a handful of the meat mixture into a sausage and place inside a cabbage leaf. Wrap the leaf around it, tucking the edges in to enclose the sausage. Lay the roll in an ovenproof dish with the seam facing down to stop it unravelling. Repeat until the meat mixture has been used up and the stuffed cabbage rolls fit snugly in the dish.

Pour the sauce over the cabbage rolls in the dish. Cover the entire dish with foil or a lid and bake in the hot oven for 1 hour or until the meat is cooked through and the cabbage leaves are tender.

Aubergine Parmigiana

Pure Italian comfort food. Aubergine parmigiana manages simultaneously to feel like peasant food and an indulgent extravagance. This beloved recipe melds velvety layers of aubergine (eggplant), a simple yet rich tomato sauce and melted mozzarella and Parmesan, all harmonising in a culinary symphony.

SERVES 6–8

4 aubergines (eggplants), sliced into
    1-cm (⅓-inch) thick rounds
1 teaspoon salt
2 tablespoons olive oil, plus extra for
    frying the aubergines
4 garlic cloves, finely chopped
1 teaspoon dried mixed herbs
2 × 400-g (14-oz) tins chopped tomatoes
1 tablespoon red wine vinegar
1 × 125-g (4½-oz) mozzarella ball
100g (3½oz) Parmesan or vegetarian
    Italian hard cheese, grated (shredded)

FOR THE CRUNCHY TOPPING (OPTIONAL)
75g (2¾oz) breadcrumbs
50g (1¾oz) Parmesan or vegetarian
    Italian hard cheese, grated (shredded)

Put the aubergines in a colander, sprinkle over the salt and shake it a little so the salt coats most of the slices. Place the colander either in the sink or set over a bowl and leave for 25 minutes so the aubergines release their liquid.

Heat the oil in a frying pan (skillet) over a gentle heat. Add the garlic and herbs and cook for 2 minutes to infuse the oil. Tip in the tinned tomatoes and vinegar, mix to combine then turn up the heat. Simmer for 30–40 minutes or until the sauce has reduced by about half.

Shake the aubergines in the colander then pat dry with kitchen paper. Heat a little oil in a separate large frying pan. Working in batches, fry the aubergine slices for a couple of minutes on each side until all the rounds are cooked. This may take up to 30 minutes. Set the cooked aubergines aside.

Preheat the oven to 180°C/160°C fan/350°F/gas 4.

Once the tomato sauce has reduced, lightly oil an ovenproof dish. Cover the base of the dish with a layer of aubergine slices, overlapping them slightly to create a full layer.

Pour over one-third of the tomato sauce, depending on the size of your dish: if you've used half of the aubergines to create the base layer, then use half of the sauce. Follow with one-third of the mozzarella and Parmesan. Repeat these layers a further one or two times until everything is used up.

I like the softness of this aubergine parmigiana, but sometimes it's nice to mix things up a bit with a crunchier topping. To make the topping, if using, combine the breadcrumbs with the Parmesan, then scatter it over the parmigiana just before baking.

Bake in the hot oven for 35–45 minutes or until the parmigiana is bubbling and the cheese is golden.

Squash, Carrot and Borlotti Tagine

Technically speaking, this is more a stew than a tagine because it's cooked in a pan rather than the type of earthenware tagine that lends the dish its name. Of course, if you have a tagine then feel free to cook it that way. This is a great dinner full of hearty vegetables that go so well with the spiced tomato sauce.

SERVES 6

1 tablespoon sunflower or vegetable oil
1 large onion, sliced
2 garlic cloves, crushed or finely grated (shredded)
1 butternut squash, peeled, deseeded and cut into bite-sized pieces
3 carrots, roughly chopped
1½ teaspoons ground cumin
1½ teaspoons ground coriander
1 teaspoon smoked paprika
1 teaspoon ground cinnamon
500ml (17fl oz) vegetable stock
1 × 400-g (14-oz) tin chopped tomatoes
2 tablespoons tomato paste (concentrated purée)
1 × 400-g (14-oz) tin borlotti beans (cranberry beans), drained and rinsed
75g (2½oz) raisins (optional)

TO SERVE
Plain couscous
Handful of chopped coriander (cilantro)

Heat the oil in a large saucepan with a lid over a medium heat. Add the onion and fry for 6–8 minutes or until beginning to brown. Stir in the garlic and cook for 1 minute, then stir in the squash and carrot and cook for a few minutes to soften.

Scatter in the spices, stir well and cook for 30 seconds before pouring in the stock and tinned tomatoes. Stir in the tomato paste, put the lid on and cook for 25 minutes.

Stir in the borlotti beans and raisins, if using, and cook with the lid on for a further 20 minutes. Check to see if the vegetables are tender and cook for a further 10–15 minutes, if necessary. If you want to thicken the sauce a little, remove the lid for the last few minutes of the cooking time.

Serve with couscous and a scattering of chopped coriander.

Spicy Mushroom Tamale Pie

The tamale pie hails from the American south and is effectively a pie with a cornbread crust. I've gone for a spicy mushroom filling with tomatoes as the base of the sauce. While it seems a lot of mushrooms, they soon cook down.

SERVES 6–8

750g (1lb 10oz) chestnut mushrooms (or wild mushrooms when available), sliced

3 tablespoons sunflower or vegetable oil

1 onion, finely chopped

4 garlic cloves, crushed or finely grated (shredded)

2 roasted red (bell) peppers from a jar, chopped

2 red chillies, finely chopped

1 teaspoon dried oregano

½ teaspoon chilli powder

150ml (5½fl oz) vegetable stock

1 × 400-g (14-oz) tin chopped tomatoes

1 × 400-g (14-oz) tin black beans, drained and rinsed

150g (5½oz) sweetcorn kernels

For the cornbread topping

225g (8oz) cornmeal or polenta

185g (6½oz) plain (all-purpose) flour

1 teaspoon baking powder

1 tablespoon sugar

225ml (8fl oz) milk

50g (1¾oz) butter, melted

3 eggs

150g (5½oz) mature Cheddar cheese, grated (shredded)

Salt and freshly ground black pepper

Preheat the oven to 200°C/180°C fan/390°F/gas 6.

Heat a large saucepan over a medium heat. Add the mushrooms and dry fry them, stirring often, until they've released their liquid and that has evaporated. Drizzle in 2 tablespoons oil and fry the mushrooms until browned. Remove the mushrooms from the pan, leaving any oil behind.

If there's less than a thin layer of oil in the pan, drizzle in another 1 tablespoon oil and fry the onion over a gentle heat for 10–12 minutes or until softened. Stir in the garlic, red peppers and chillies and cook for a few minutes more. Stir in the oregano, chilli powder and a good seasoning of salt and pepper, cook for 30 seconds and then return the mushrooms to the pan. Stir everything together.

Pour in the stock, tinned tomatoes and black beans and cook for 5–10 minutes or until the sauce has thickened. Stir through the sweetcorn kernels and then tip the filling into a large ovenproof dish. Set aside.

Make the cornbread topping by combining the cornmeal, flour, baking powder and sugar in a bowl. Pour the milk and melted butter into a jug (pitcher), then beat in the eggs and season with salt and pepper. Tip the milk mixture into the dry ingredients and stir until just combined, then mix through the cheese.

Spoon the cornbread topping on top of the mushroom filling and then level the surface. Bake the pie in the hot oven for 25–30 minutes or until a skewer inserted into the cornbread topping comes out clean.

Cook's tip Julia Child insisted on not crowding the pan when cooking mushrooms until golden. As there are so many here, I chuck them all in at once. To ensure the mushrooms brown properly, wait until the liquid has been released and evaporated before adding oil.

Midweek Meals

Cottage Pie

I was once told that cottage pie was so called because it had a sliced potato top that made it look like the roof of a cottage, while shepherd's pie has a mashed potato top. I actually find it easier to mash the potatoes than slice them up, but feel free to do either.

SERVES 6-8

2 tablespoons vegetable oil
1kg (2lb 4oz) minced (ground) beef
2 onions, chopped
2 carrots, chopped (I cut these bigger
   than a usual sofrito to add texture)
2 celery sticks, chopped
2 garlic cloves, chopped or crushed
1 tablespoon dried mixed herbs
2 tablespoons tomato paste
   (concentrated purée)
2 × 400-g (14-oz) tins chopped tomatoes
200ml (7fl oz) red wine
1 tablespoon Worcestershire sauce
   (gluten-free, if necessary)
1 beef stock cube
200g (7oz) frozen peas
Salt and freshly ground black pepper

FOR THE POTATO TOPPING

1kg (2lb 4oz) Maris Piper potatoes, peeled
   and quartered
75ml (2½fl oz) milk
A good knob of butter
75g (2½oz) Cheddar cheese, grated
   (shredded)

Warm 1 tablespoon oil in a large saucepan over a high heat. Add the beef and cook until brown. Remove the pan from the heat and transfer the meat to a large bowl using a slotted spoon. Leaving 1 tablespoon fat in the pan, drain the rest away.

Drizzle the remaining oil into the pan. Add the onion, carrot and celery and cook over a medium heat for 10 minutes or until softened but not too brown. Stir in the garlic and herbs and cook for a further 1 minute. Add the tomato paste and tinned tomatoes. Fill the tin with water and add that to the pan with the red wine, Worcestershire sauce and stock cube. Season with salt and pepper. Simmer for 30 minutes or until the carrots are tender and the liquid has thickened. You want a thick liquid, so you don't end up with a watery sauce.

Meanwhile, make the potato topping. Boil the potatoes in a pan of salted water until tender and knife easily breaks them apart. Drain the potatoes, return them to the pan and mash with a potato ricer. Add the milk, butter, a pinch of salt and plenty of pepper and stir to combine. Set aside.

Preheat the oven to 200°C/180°C fan/390°F/gas 6.

Stir the frozen peas into the beef mixture, then spoon it into an ovenproof dish, leaving at gap of a few centimetres (an inch) between the mixture and the lip of the dish. Top the pie with the mashed potato then scatter over the Cheddar. Bake in the preheated oven for 20–30 minutes or until the cheese has melted and the top is golden.

Got leftovers? If your dish isn't large enough to hold all the pie mixture, any leftover cooked beef can be frozen for up to 3 months. Defrost the mixture fully before topping with mashed potato and baking. Alternatively, make up a full pie in a freezer-safe, ovenproof dish, cover and freeze. The pie can be cooked from frozen – this takes 45–60 minutes as the pie needs to be piping hot all the way through before serving.

Sloppy Joes

These meat sandwiches are an American classic. Featuring that well-known barbecue flavour, which is characteristic of many staple dishes from the US, Sloppy Joes are a great crowd pleaser. They're perfect for when you want to get everyone involved around the dinner table.

SERVES 4 OR 8

1 tablespoon oil
1 onion, chopped
2 garlic cloves, crushed or finely chopped
1 red (bell) pepper, chopped
1 yellow (bell) pepper, chopped
500g (1lb 2oz) minced (ground) beef
1 × 400-g (14-oz) tin chopped tomatoes
90ml (6 tablespoons) barbecue sauce
A few splashes of Worcestershire sauce
2 tablespoons tomato paste (concentrated purée)
½–1 teaspoon chilli powder (optional)
2 tablespoons brown sugar
1 beef stock cube

TO SERVE
8 burger buns, halved and toasted
Cheddar cheese, grated (shredded)

Over a medium heat, drizzle the oil into a large frying pan (skillet) or saucepan and fry the onion until soft, around 6–8 minutes. Tip in the garlic and both red and yellow peppers and cook for a further 5 minutes until the peppers have softened. Mix in the beef and cook for a few minutes until browned.

Pour in the tinned tomatoes and stir in the barbecue sauce, Worcestershire sauce, tomato paste, chilli power, if using, brown sugar and stock cube. Bring to a simmer and cook for about 15 minutes until the sauce has thickened and is not at all watery. Serve the mixture in the burger buns with grated Cheddar.

Make it smoky If you prefer a smokier barbecue flavour, try adding 2 teaspoons smoked paprika to the beef mixture when you add the chilli powder.

Chicken Paprikash

I love paprika. Lucky, really, because it goes so well with tomatoes. Combining paprika, tomatoes and sour cream delivers a warming, cheerful sauce which is the perfect companion to chicken. I like to serve this with brown rice, but it also goes great with potatoes, too.

SERVES 4

1–2 tablespoons sunflower or vegetable oil
1kg (2lb 4oz) bone-in, skin-on chicken thighs
1 onion, sliced
1 red (bell) pepper, chopped
1 garlic clove, crushed or finely chopped
2 tablespoons sweet smoked paprika
1 × 400-g (14-oz) tin chopped tomatoes
250ml (9fl oz) chicken stock (gluten-free, if necessary)
150ml (5½fl oz) sour cream
Salt and freshly ground black pepper

TO SERVE

Plain cooked brown rice or boiled potatoes

Heat the oil in a large saucepan or frying pan (skillet) with a lid over a medium heat. Put the chicken thighs in the pan, skin side down, then season and fry for a few minutes to brown. Flip the chicken over, season the other side and cook for a few more minutes until the chicken is browned all over. Remove the chicken from the pan and set aside.

Tip the onion and red pepper into the pan and fry for 6–8 minutes or until softened and beginning to brown. Stir in the garlic and cook for 1 minute before adding the paprika. Stir well before pouring in the tinned tomatoes and stock. Season well, return the chicken to the pan, pop on the lid and cook for 10 minutes.

Remove the lid and cook for a further 10–15 minutes or until the chicken is cooked through. (At this point, I sometimes turn over any large chicken thighs to help them along.) Spoon in the sour cream, mix around the sauce and cook for 2 minutes.

Serve with brown rice or boiled potatoes.

Storage You can store this chicken paprikash in the fridge for a few days or keep it in the freezer for up to 3 months. If freezing, do not add the sour cream before storing. When ready to serve, defrost the chicken paprikash if frozen, then reheat it until piping hot throughout. It should reach 70°C/160°F on a probe thermometer. Stir through the sour cream before serving.

Sausage Casserole with Cheesy Polenta

A hearty stew puts smiles on faces, especially as nights grow colder. The joy of a sausage stew is that you don't have to wait for the meat to tenderise or fall off the bone. It usually makes the dish much cheaper, too. Tinned tomatoes are another easy way to make a stew flavoursome without having to simmer it away for hours. Once again, you can count on the trusty tin of tomatoes!

SERVES 4–6

500g (1lb 2oz) chestnut mushrooms, sliced

2–3 tablespoons olive oil

8 good-quality pork sausages

1 large onion, sliced

1 red (bell) pepper, chopped

2 garlic cloves, crushed or finely grated (shredded)

1 tablespoon dried mixed herbs

1 × 400-g (14-oz) tin chopped tomatoes or plum tomatoes

1 tablespoon tomato paste (concentrated purée)

1 chicken or vegetable stock cube

125g (4½oz) dried red lentils, rinsed

FOR THE CHEESY POLENTA

400ml (14fl oz) milk

150g (5½oz) quick-cook polenta

40g (1½oz) Parmesan cheese, grated (shredded)

25g (¾oz) butter

Heat a large saucepan over a medium heat and dry fry the mushrooms until their water has released and evaporated. Drizzle in 1 tablespoon olive oil and brown the mushrooms. Use a slotted spoon to transfer the mushrooms to a bowl, leaving as much of the oil behind as possible.

Next, add the sausages to the pan and fry until browned all over. Remove the sausages from the pan and set aside with the mushrooms. If there's a layer of oil still remaining, simply tip in the onion, otherwise drizzle in another 1 tablespoon oil. Fry the onion for 8–10 minutes or until softened, then stir in the red pepper and fry for 5 minutes. Add the garlic and fry for 1 minute.

Scatter in the mixed herbs, season well with salt and pepper, stir everything around and add the tinned tomatoes, 1½ tins water, tomato paste, stock cube and lentils. Return the mushrooms and sausages to the pan, bring to a simmer and cook for 20–25 minutes or until the lentils are tender and the sauce has thickened.

About 10 minutes before the stew is ready, make the polenta. Pour 500ml (17fl oz) water into a saucepan and add the milk. Bring to a simmer then gradually sprinkle in the polenta, whisking continuously to ensure it doesn't go lumpy. Cook for up to 5 minutes until thickened. Scatter in the Parmesan, tip in the butter and mix everything to combine until the butter and cheese have both melted.

Serve the stew over the polenta.

Meatballs and Spaghetti

If I ever go to New York City, this is exactly what I hope to eat: the classic Italian-American dish of meatballs and spaghetti all doused in tomato sauce. Combining cumin and tomatoes is a revelation; they pair so well here.

SERVES 4–6

1 tablespoon olive oil
16–20 good-quality meatballs
(store-bought or homemade,
see opposite)
400g (14oz) dried spaghetti
50g (1¾oz) Parmesan cheese
Handful of torn basil leaves, to serve
(optional)

FOR THE SAUCE

2 tablespoons olive oil
1 onion, finely chopped
1 carrot, grated (shredded)
1 tablespoon dried mixed herbs
4 garlic cloves, crushed
1 teaspoon paprika
1 teaspoon cumin
1 × 400-g (14-oz) tin chopped tomatoes
1 tablespoon tomato paste
(concentrated purée)
1 teaspoon Worcestershire sauce
1 tablespoon red wine vinegar
Salt and freshly ground black pepper

Meatball subs Drop the spaghetti and swap it for 4 medium baguettes. Cook the sauce down a little more so that it's thicker and not at all runny. Ladle a few spoonfuls of sauce into each baguette, fill with meatballs and grate over plenty of Parmesan.

To make your own meatballs, fry 1 very finely chopped onion (it's important to chop it super fine to ensure the meatballs don't break up) in 1 teaspoon oil until the onion is softened and beginning to brown. Allow to cool for 10–15 minutes. Combine the onion with 800g (1lb 12oz) minced (ground) beef, 50g (1¾ oz) panko or fresh breadcrumbs, 1 egg, 1 tablespoon dried mixed herbs, 1 crushed or finely grated garlic clove and plenty of salt and pepper in a large bowl. Mix everything together well – I find it's easiest to get your hands in and smush it all between your fingers. Shape the mixture into 20 equal-sized meatballs.

Heat the olive oil in a large non-stick frying pan (skillet) or saucepan with a lid over a medium heat. Add the meatballs and fry until browned all over; they don't need to be cooked all the way through. Remove the meatballs from the pan and set aside. If your pan isn't non-stick, you may wish to clean it at this point.

To make the sauce, warm the oil in the pan over a gentle heat. Add the onion, carrot and herbs and fry with the lid on for 10 minutes or until soft. Stir in the garlic and cook for 1 minute. Add the paprika and cumin and cook for 1 minute. Pour in the tinned tomatoes, plus around ¼ tin water. Add the tomato paste, Worcestershire sauce and vinegar. Season well, stir everything together and cook for 5 minutes.

Add the meatballs back into the pan – ideally in one layer, but if you need to stack a few it'll be fine as they will shrink a little more. Cover and cook for 10 minutes, then remove the lid and cook for a further 10 minutes to thicken the sauce.

In the final 10 minutes, cook the spaghetti according to the packet instructions. Drain the spaghetti, reserving a little of the cooking water. Take around a cupful of tomato sauce from the meatballs and stir it through the spaghetti in the pan, adding a splash of the cooking water.

Divide the spaghetti between serving bowls and top with the meatballs and remaining sauce. Grate over some Parmesan and garnish with a few basil leaves, if using.

Pizza Sliders

A simple way to change up the standard pizza, these are great for a kids' party or for a movie night with friends. You can even throw in a couple of ingredients like jalapeños or anchovies to make them feel a little more grown up.

MAKES 6

6 white bread rolls
6 pepperoni slices
3 ham slices
1 × 125-g (4½-oz) mozzarella ball
75g (2½oz) Cheddar cheese, grated
  (shredded)

FOR THE PIZZA SAUCE

½ tablespoon olive oil
1 garlic clove, crushed or finely grated
  (shredded)
1 × 227-g (8-oz) tin chopped tomatoes
1 teaspoon dried oregano
Salt and freshly ground black pepper

Preheat the oven to 220°C/200°C fan/430°F/gas 7.

To make the pizza sauce, heat the oil in a frying pan (skillet) over a low heat and fry the garlic for a couple of minutes until softened. Tip in the tinned tomatoes and scatter in the oregano. Season with salt and freshly ground black pepper and cook for 10 minutes over a medium-low heat to thicken the tomatoes. Leave to cool a little and then blend, if you like a smoother sauce.

Cut the bread rolls in half. (If I can, I buy a pack of 6 rolls that are all attached at the base, then I slice them open so that the bottom halves remain attached when I bake them – it makes things feel a little snazzier.) Put the bottom halves of the rolls in a roasting tin (sheet pan).

Spread the pizza sauce over the bottom halves of the rolls. Top 3 of the rolls with pepperoni and 3 of the rolls with ham. Tear the mozzarella over all the rolls and top each one with the grated Cheddar. Tuck the tops of the rolls around the edges of the tray.

Bake the sliders in the hot oven for 15–20 minutes or until the rolls have browned and the cheese is golden. If the tops look like they're browning too much, you can take them out of the oven sooner.

Remove the sliders from the oven and squidge the tops of the rolls onto the bottom halves before serving.

Flavour combos This recipe for Pizza Sliders gives you a couple of options for flavour combinations, but of course you can swap out the pepperoni or ham for whatever you like. Or you can build the sliders up further by adding ingredients such as baby spinach leaves, roasted vegetables, artichokes from a jar or even, dare I say it, pineapple chunks with the ham.

Chorizo and Potato Hash

This brunch dish is a spin on the hash we always enjoyed at our favourite local café, Robinsons, when we lived in York — just one of the places that was incredibly passionate about good produce and served up dishes that kept you going back again and again. We went *countless* times with friends and always ordered this dish. As well as the 2-for-1 mimosas.

SERVES 2

350g (12½oz) leftover boiled potatoes, chopped into bite-sized pieces or uncooked and cooked at the start
2 tablespoons olive oil, plus extra for frying the eggs (if necessary)
1 red onion, sliced
125g (4½oz) chorizo, chopped
2 thyme sprigs
1 teaspoon smoked paprika
1 × 227-g (8-oz) tin chopped tomatoes
2–4 eggs
Salt and freshly ground black pepper

TO SERVE

1½ tablespoons pumpkin seeds (pepitas)
2 teaspoons nigella seeds (optional)
Thick slices of sourdough toast (optional)

If you're not using left-over boiled potatoes, chop the uncooked potatoes into bite-sized pieces and boil in salt water for 15 minutes until tender. Drain and set aside to dry out a little.

Heat 1 tablespoon oil in a large frying pan (skillet) over a medium heat. Add the onion and fry for 8–10 minutes or until beginning to brown and caramelize a little. Tip in the potatoes, drizzle in another 1 tablespoon oil and cook for 5 minutes to brown. Stir often to make sure the onion doesn't burn.

Stir in the chorizo, thyme sprigs and paprika and fry for 4–5 minutes to release the oils and colour the potatoes.

Pour in the tinned tomatoes, season really well with salt and freshly ground black pepper and cook for 5 minutes to thicken.

Poach or fry the eggs to your preference. Serve the eggs on top of or alongside the hash, removing the thyme just before plating up. Scatter over the pumpkin seeds and nigella seeds, if using, and serve with toasted sourdough, if you like.

Storage You can store this chorizo and potato hash in the fridge for a few days or keep it in the freezer for up to 3 months. When ready to serve, defrost the hash if frozen and reheat it until piping hot throughout. Poach or fry the eggs just before serving.

Cheat's Chicken Pomodoro

Traditionally made with fresh cherry tomatoes, this dish makes a great speedy dinner. If you're cooking for two, this recipe is easily halved or leftovers can be frozen to enjoy on another day. Try serving with brown rice, potatoes or polenta.

SERVES 4

4 skinless chicken breasts
2 teaspoons dried Italian herbs
2 tablespoons olive oil
1 onion, chopped
4 garlic cloves, crushed or finely grated
   (shredded)
125ml (4fl oz) white wine
250ml (8fl oz) chicken stock
1 tablespoon red wine vinegar
1 × 400-g (14-oz) tin chopped tomatoes
   or cherry tomatoes
Salt and freshly ground black pepper

TO SERVE
Handful of torn basil leaves
25g (¾oz) Parmesan cheese, shaved
   or grated (shredded)

Season the chicken with salt, pepper and 1 teaspoon dried herbs. Heat 1 tablespoon oil in a large frying pan (skillet) and fry the chicken on each side for 2–3 minutes until lightly golden but not cooked through. Remove from the pan and set aside.

Drizzle the remaining oil into the same frying pan and fry the onion for 6–8 minutes over a medium-low heat to soften and allow to golden a little. Stir in the garlic and cook for 1 minute, ensuring it doesn't burn. Pour in the wine, stock and vinegar, then cook for 5 minutes before adding the tinned tomatoes, remaining dried herbs and a good pinch of salt and freshly ground black pepper.

Return the chicken to the pan. Cook for 10–15 minutes until the sauce has thickened (it should be quite thick, rather than a really thin sauce) and the chicken is cooked through.

Scatter over the torn basil leaves and serve with Parmesan, if you like.

Tuna Pasta Bake

Before I met my partner, Gareth, I made tuna pasta bake with a white sauce. Oh, how wrong I was! The tuna-tomato combo has a much better flavour and texture, not to mention a far better nutritional profile. To my mind, the cheese topping is non-negotiable. The breadcrumbs, on the other hand, can be omitted. Be warned though, you'll miss out on the crunch as your spoon dives through.

SERVES 4–6

50–75g (1¾–2½oz) panko breadcrumbs (optional)

100g (3½oz) Cheddar cheese, grated (shredded)

Half a small bunch of parsley, leaves and stalks separated, both chopped

400g (14oz) dried pasta (penne, fusilli or rigatoni all work well)

½ tablespoon sunflower or vegetable oil

1 red onion, chopped

1 red (bell) pepper, chopped

1 × 400-g (14-oz) tin chopped tomatoes

1 tablespoon tomato paste (concentrated purée)

1 teaspoon dried mixed herbs

2 × 145-g (5½oz) tins tuna in spring water, drained

100g (3½oz) sweetcorn kernels (optional)

Salt and freshly ground black pepper

Preheat the oven to 200°C/180°C fan/390°F/gas 6.

To make the crumb topping, combine the breadcrumbs and cheese in a small bowl with half the chopped parsley leaves and set aside. The amount of breadcrumbs needed will depend on the size of your ovenproof dish, so a wider, shallower dish with more surface area will require more crumb topping.

Bring a large saucepan of salted water to the boil. Add the pasta to the pan and boil for 6–8 minutes (or 2 minutes less than given in the packet instructions) or until almost tender. Once cooked, drain, reserving a mugful of the pasta cooking water, then set aside.

Heat the oil in the same pan over a medium heat. Add the onion, red pepper and parsley stalks, if using, with a pinch of salt and fry for 6–8 minutes or until softened. Mix in the tinned tomatoes, tomato paste and dried herbs. Fry for a few minutes before adding the remaining parsley leaves and tuna. Cook for a few minutes to heat through then tip in the sweetcorn, if using, and season well with salt and freshly ground black pepper.

Combine the pasta and sauce, adding a little of the pasta cooking water if needed. Tip the pasta mixture into an ovenproof dish and scatter the crumb topping over the top, if using. Alternatively, cover the top with a scattering of Cheddar. Bake in the hot oven for 20–30 minutes or until the top is golden.

Cook's note I usually prepare my pasta bakes in a large ovenproof pan so that I can cook the sauce, pasta and then bake all in the same pan. Simply cook the pasta in the ovenproof saucepan, drain, then set aside while you make the sauce.

Prawn and Coconut Curry

Having a quick curry recipe in your repertoire is ideal for when you fancy a spicier midweek meal or when you want to entertain with minimum fuss. The speedy cooking of prawns (shrimps) lends itself to quicker meals; they really do cook in just a few minutes, so don't be tempted to give them any longer. If you want to make an evening that little bit special, serve with rice or naan breads, poppadoms, raita and your favourite chutneys.

SERVES 4

1 tablespoon sunflower or vegetable oil
1 large red onion, sliced
Thumb-sized piece (about 25g/¾oz)
   of fresh root ginger, finely chopped
   or grated (shredded)
2 large garlic cloves, finely chopped
   or grated (shredded)
1 red chilli, sliced (omit if you prefer
   a mild curry)
4 tablespoons balti spice paste
   (gluten-free, if necessary)
1 × 400-g (14-oz) tin chopped tomatoes
1 × 400-ml (14-fl oz) tin coconut milk
300g (10½oz) raw prawns (shrimp),
   cleaned and deveined

TO SERVE
Handful of torn coriander (cilantro) leaves
1 lime, cut into wedges
Plain cooked rice or naan bread (optional)
Poppadoms (optional)
Your choice of raita or chutneys

Drizzle the oil into a large frying pan (skillet) or saucepan and heat over a medium-low heat. Add the onion with a pinch of salt and fry for 6–8 minutes until soft. Stir in the ginger, garlic and chilli and cook for 1–2 minutes to soften slightly, ensuring the garlic doesn't burn.

Mix in the balti spice paste with a splash of water (I usually find 1 tablespoon is enough) and cook for 2–3 minutes to unleash the flavour.

Pour in the tinned tomatoes and coconut milk and simmer gently for 8–10 minutes to thicken slightly. (Meanwhile, this is a good moment to start cooking your rice.)

Scatter in the prawns and gently stir them into the sauce. Cook the prawns for 3–4 minutes only until pink and just cooked. You really don't want to overcook them because the joy of prawns is in their firm but bouncy texture.

Scatter over the torn coriander and a bright squeeze of lime. Serve the curry with your choice of plain rice or naan bread, poppadoms and any raita or chutneys on the side.

Lovely additions This is a great simple curry, but if you'd like to add some extra veg then spinach and green beans both work well. Spinach leaves can be stirred into the curry with the prawns and allowed to wilt and green beans can be added a couple of minutes before the prawns are added.

Easy Chana Masala

Chana masala is a North Indian chickpea (garbanzo bean) curry that traditionally uses soaked dried chickpeas, however, using tinned ones gives you the flexibility to make this dish quickly. Tomatoes and chickpeas are a great combination, especially when enveloped in spices.

SERVES 4

2 tablespoons sunflower or vegetable oil
1 large onion, finely chopped
4 garlic cloves, crushed or finely grated (shredded)
Thumb-sized piece of fresh root ginger, finely grated (shredded)
2 green chillies, finely chopped
½ tablespoon ground coriander
½ tablespoon ground cumin
½ teaspoon chilli powder
½ teaspoon ground turmeric
½ teaspoon garam masala
1 × 400-g (14-oz) tin chopped tomatoes
1 tablespoon tomato paste (concentrated purée)
1 × 400-g (14-oz) tin chickpeas (garbanzo beans), drained and rinsed
Juice of ½ lemon

TO SERVE
Handful of chopped coriander (cilantro)
Plain cooked rice or roti

Heat the oil in a large frying pan (skillet) or saucepan over a gentle heat. Add the onion and fry until softened, around 10–12 minutes. Stir in the garlic, ginger and green chillies, then cook for a further 1 minute.

Sprinkle in the spices, stir everything together and cook for 30 seconds. Tip in the tomatoes, half a tin of water, the tomato paste and chickpeas. Cook for 20–30 minutes over a low heat to thicken the sauce and until the chickpeas are tender.

Stir in the lemon juice and scatter over the coriander before serving with rice or roti.

Easy Ratatouille

This is not the ratatouille you may recall from the Disney movie, where vegetables are cut into paper-thin slices and baked in concentric circles. Instead, I prefer to chop everything into chunks and cook it on the hob (stovetop) so it's saucier. That way, it can be used for a range of dishes or served on its own as the champion on the plate. Try spooning the ratatouille onto slices of toasted bread and topping with marinated anchovies to create Basque-style pintxos.

SERVES 4-6

4 tablespoons olive oil
2 onions, chopped
2 red (bell) peppers, roughly chopped
2 aubergines (eggplants), roughly chopped
2 courgettes (zucchini), roughly chopped
2 × 400-g (14-oz) tins chopped tomatoes
1 tablespoon dried herbes de Provence
2 bay leaves
Salt and freshly ground black pepper
Handful of torn basil leaves, to serve

Heat 2 tablespoons oil in a large saucepan with a lid. Add the onions and red peppers and fry for 6–8 minutes or until soft and beginning to golden. Remove from the pan then set aside.

Heat the remaining oil in the pan. Tip in the aubergines and courgettes, then cook for 12–15 minutes or until softened and beginning to golden.

Return the onions and red peppers to the pan along with the tinned tomatoes, dried herbs, bay leaves and a good seasoning of salt and pepper. Simmer for 10 minutes, covering the pan with the lid if the ratatouille starts to dry out too much.

Remove the bay leaves, then serve the ratatouille garnished with the torn basil leaves.

Storing and reheating This ratatouille will store quite happily in the fridge for a few days. Reheat until piping hot throughout. Although it's fine to freeze this dish (it'll freeze for up to 3 months), because of the high water content of the vegetables, you may find the texture of the ratatouille becomes a little more mushy once defrosted and reheated.

Minestrone

I think of minestrone as a cross between a soup and a stew. Maybe because it's not blitzed, but mostly because it feels so hearty and comforting – like a big hug from your favourite Auntie. The tinned tomatoes bring all the vegetables to life in this Roman classic. While I like including small pasta shapes, such as macaroni, you can use other types of pasta. You can even break up any odds and ends of spaghetti to make it more like the classic tinned version.

SERVES 6

1½ tablespoons olive oil
1 onion, finely chopped
1 celery stick, finely chopped
1 small leek, finely chopped
1 carrot, finely chopped
1 large courgette (zucchini), finely
   chopped
2 garlic cloves, crushed
½ teaspoon dried Italian herbs
2 tablespoons tomato paste
   (concentrated purée)
1½ litres (48fl oz) vegetable stock
2 bay leaves
1 × 400-g (14-oz) tin chopped tomatoes
1 × 400-g (14-oz) tin cannellini beans,
   drained and rinsed
100g (3½oz) dried macaroni pasta
150g (5½oz) green beans, chopped
100g (3½oz) kale or cavolo nero, chopped
Salt and freshly ground black pepper

TO SERVE
Handful of torn basil leaves
25g (¾oz) Parmesan or vegetarian or
   vegan Italian hard cheese, grated
   (shredded)

Heat the oil in a large pan over a gentle heat. Add the onion, celery, leek and carrot and fry until softened but not golden, around 8–10 minutes. Add the courgette and cook for a further 5 minutes, again until softened. Stir in the garlic and dried herbs and cook for 1 minute more.

Squeeze in the tomato paste, pour in the stock and toss in the bay leaves. Tip in the tinned tomatoes and cannellini beans, along with the macaroni pasta and cook for 10–15 minutes or until the pasta is almost tender.

Season well with salt and freshly ground black pepper, then tip in the green beans and kale and cook for 2–3 minutes or until the green beans are tender. I like my minestrone chunky, but if you prefer a thinner soup then you can add 100–200ml (3½–7fl oz) more hot water.

Remove the bay leaves, then serve with a scattering of basil leaves and a little grated (shredded) Parmesan or hard cheese, if you like.

Homemade 'Baked' Beans

I love tinned baked beans on toast with lashings of grated (shredded) Cheddar cheese and a squirt of brown sauce. Even better are homemade baked beans, which you can easily change up with additions like chorizo and Barbecue Sauce (page 151) or by upping the smoked paprika. As well as being great on toast, these beans are just as good served in a classic baked potato.

SERVES 4 GENEROUSLY

½ tablespoon sunflower or vegetable oil
1 small red onion, very finely chopped
1 garlic clove, crushed or finely grated (shredded)
½ teaspoon smoked paprika
½ teaspoon dried mixed herbs
1 × 400-g (14-oz) tin chopped tomatoes
1 tablespoon tomato paste (concentrated purée)
1 tablespoon maple syrup
1 teaspoon Worcestershire sauce (use the vegan version if you need this dish to be vegetarian or vegan)
2 × 400-g (14-oz) tins haricot beans (navy beans), drained and rinsed

Heat the oil in a saucepan over a medium-low heat. Add the onion with a pinch of salt and fry for 8–10 minutes, until soft but not golden. Tip in the garlic, paprika and mixed herbs and cook for 1 minute.

Stir in the tinned tomatoes, tomato paste, maple syrup and Worcestershire sauce. Cook for 5 minutes before tipping in the beans and half a tin of water and cooking for a further 45 minutes–1 hour or until the beans are tender and the sauce has thickened. You may also notice that the sauce changes from a deep red to more of an orange colour.

Storing and reheating These beans will keep quite happily in the fridge for a few days or in the freezer for up to 3 months. If frozen, defrost fully before reheating until piping hot throughout. Try freezing the beans in tin-sized batches so that you've got exactly the right amount to hand each time.

Snacks, Sides and Sauces

Tomato Ketchup

I love a homemade tomato ketchup; it feels decadent and has a much more grown-up flavour than any ketchup you can buy ready-made. That's not to say there's no place for the classic ketchup, but this one is great with a home-cooked fry-up or with your bangers and mash.

MAKES AROUND 375ML (13FL OZ)

2 teaspoons sunflower or vegetable oil
1 small onion, chopped
1 celery stick, chopped
1 garlic clove, crushed or finely chopped
¼ teaspoon ground cloves
½ teaspoon ground allspice
½ teaspoon ground cinnamon
1 × 400-g (14-oz) tin chopped tomatoes
    or plum tomatoes
1 tablespoon tomato paste
    (concentrated purée)
75ml (2½fl oz) red wine vinegar
2 tablespoons malt vinegar
50g (1¾oz) soft light brown sugar
¼ teaspoon English mustard
1 bay leaf
Salt and freshly ground black pepper

Heat the oil in a saucepan over a gentle heat. Add the onion and celery and fry for 10–12 minutes or until softened. Stir in the garlic, cook for 1 minute, then stir in the spices and cook for 30 seconds.

Tip in the tinned tomatoes and tomato paste, then pour in both vinegars. Season well with salt and pepper then stir in the sugar, mustard and bay leaf. Bring to a simmer and cook for 15–20 minutes or until much thicker.

Remove the bay leaf and blend until smooth. If you like a super-smooth ketchup, you can strain through a fine-mesh sieve (strainer) into a bowl. If it's too thin after sieving, simmer for up to 20 minutes longer to reduce further. If you do this, it will make less than the amount stated above.

Pour the ketchup into a sterilised jar or bottle and keep for up to 3 months in the fridge.

Movie-Night Salsa

A salsa dip is the ultimate party-night snack. While ready-made versions aren't too expensive, the list of ingredients and additives are staggering. It's so easy to make your own. I like to go for plain chopped tomatoes or plum tomatoes, so they retain a bit of texture. Tortilla chips and breadsticks advised!

SERVES 4–8

½ small red onion or 1 shallot
1 small green (bell) pepper, deseeded
Handful of chopped coriander (cilantro)
1 × 400-g (14-oz) tin chopped tomatoes
2 teaspoons olive oil
Juice of ½ lime
1 teaspoon red wine vinegar
Salt and freshly ground black pepper

Put the onion, pepper and coriander in a food processor and pulse a few times to finely chop.

Tip in the tinned tomatoes and drizzle in the olive oil, lime juice and red wine vinegar. Season well with salt and freshly ground black pepper and pulse a few more times.

Pour into your serving bowl and serve with tortilla chips or breadsticks, if you like.

Barbecue Sauce

Ideal for serving with burgers, hot dogs or chicken wings, and for marinating meats and veg, there is a wide spectrum of barbecue sauces available. This one is zingy and sweet, making the most of the natural tinned tomato flavours.

MAKES 500ML (17FL OZ)

½ tablespoon oil
1 onion, chopped
1 × 400-g (14-oz) tin chopped tomatoes
 or plum tomatoes
4 tablespoons malt vinegar
50g (1¾oz) soft dark brown sugar
1 teaspoon English mustard
1 teaspoon Worcestershire sauce
½ teaspoon garlic granules
1 teaspoon smoked paprika (optional)
Juice of ½ lemon

Heat the oil in a saucepan over a gentle heat and fry the onions for 10–12 minutes or until softened but not golden.

Tip in all the remaining ingredients except the lemon juice and simmer for around 20 minutes or until much thickened.

Season, blend until smooth then drizzle in the lemon juice and stir. Pour into a sterilised jar or bottle and keep for up to 3 months in the fridge.

Spicy Tomato Salsa

For a more grown-up salsa, chilli really lifts things. You can, of course, add more or less chilli to work with your preferred spice level, but this one gives you a mild to medium heat depending on the potency of your green chilli. This salsa is great served with potato crisps (chips), as part of a salad or in a spicy fajita.

SERVES 4–6

2 tablespoons olive oil
4 garlic cloves, peeled
1 green chilli, roughly chopped
Half a small bunch of coriander (cilantro), roughly chopped
1 × 400-g (14-oz) tin plum tomatoes
1 tablespoon tomato paste (concentrated purée)
1 tablespoon soft light brown sugar
Salt and freshly ground black pepper

Put the olive oil, garlic, green chilli and coriander in a food processor and blitz until finely chopped but not a paste.

Tip in the tinned tomatoes, tomato paste and sugar. Season with salt and pepper and pulse another couple of times.

Hot Sauce

There are many types of hot sauce, this one is similar to an American-style sauce. It's spicy, but also has a sweetness thanks to the apple juice and sugar.

MAKES 700ML (24FL OZ)

2 teaspoons oil
2 onions, finely chopped
2 garlic cloves, crushed or finely grated (shredded)
10 red chillies, finely chopped
1 × 400-g (14-oz) tin chopped tomatoes
150ml (5½fl oz) red wine vinegar
200ml (7fl oz) apple juice
40g (1½oz) granulated white sugar

Drizzle the oil into a saucepan and warm over a gentle heat. Add the onion and fry until softened but not golden, around 10–12 minutes. Stir in the garlic and chilli and cook for a further 5 minutes until also softened.

Stir in the tinned tomatoes, vinegar, apple juice and sugar and simmer for 15–20 minutes or until thickened slightly. Season well with salt and pepper, cool a little then blend everything together until smooth.

Decant into a sterilised jar or bottle. This sauce will keep for a few weeks when stored in the fridge.

Peperonata

Slow-cooked peppers in tomato sauce are a great accompaniment to meats, but also work well in a summer salad. Feel free to serve either hot or cold.

SERVES 4 AS A SIDE

2 tablespoons olive oil
2 onions, sliced
2 garlic cloves, crushed or finely grated (shredded)
2 red (bell) peppers, sliced
2 yellow (bell) peppers, sliced
1 × 227-g (7-oz) tin chopped tomatoes, plum tomatoes or cherry tomatoes
½ tablespoon red wine vinegar
1 teaspoon granulated white sugar
A few fresh oregano sprigs or ½ teaspoon dried oregano
Salt and freshly ground black pepper

Heat the oil in a large saucepan with a lid over a gentle heat. Add the onions and fry for 10–12 minutes or until softened but not golden. Stir in the garlic, cook for 1 minute, then add both red and yellow peppers and stir well. Put the lid on the pan and cook for 20–30 minutes over a low heat until the peppers have softened.

Remove the lid then pour in the tinned tomatoes and vinegar, then stir in the sugar and oregano. Season well with salt and pepper. Simmer gently for 30–40 minutes or until the peppers are very soft but still hold their shape. Remove the lid, if there's a lot of watery liquid at the bottom you can simmer for a further 5–10 minutes to reduce it or you can serve as is. Remove the oregano sprigs before serving, if you used them.

Makhani Sauce

This is a great basic curry sauce to have up your sleeve to elevate your Friday-night fakeaways. Or you can make a ready-to-indulge batch and keep it in the freezer. Tinned tomatoes are the base ingredient for several curries as they go well with the spices and enhance the colour of the dish.

SERVES 4

3 tablespoons vegetable oil
1 onion, sliced
4 garlic cloves, crushed or finely grated (shredded)
Thumb-sized piece of fresh root ginger, finely grated (shredded)
1 teaspoon chilli powder
1 teaspoon ground cumin
1 teaspoon ground coriander
2 teaspoons garam masala
1 × 400-g (14-oz) tin chopped tomatoes or plum tomatoes
2 tablespoons cashew butter or 50g (1¾oz) cashews, blended to a fine paste (optional)
2 teaspoons granulated white sugar
4–6 tablespoons double (heavy) cream
Handful of chopped coriander (cilantro), to serve

Heat the oil in a frying pan (skillet) or saucepan over a medium heat. Add the onion and fry until soft and beginning to brown, about 6–8 minutes. Stir in the garlic and ginger and cook for a couple of minutes before stirring in the spices. Cook for 1 minute.

Stir in the tinned tomatoes, breaking them up with a wooden spoon if using plum tomatoes, along with half a tinful of water and followed by the cashew butter and sugar. Cook for 20–30 minutes or until thickened.

Add 4 tablespoons of the cream and stir through. Taste the sauce and decide whether you'd like the sauce to be creamier. If so, add the remaining 2 tablespoons of cream.

Scatter over the chopped coriander before serving.

Make it your way If you want to add chicken, lamb or beef then brown the meat before cooking the onion, remove it from the pan and add it back in when you pour in the tinned tomatoes. For those skipping the meat, try chickpeas (garbanzo beans) or roasted butternut squash to bulk it up. Spinach is always a good choice for a bit of veg in a curry too.

Basic Curry Sauce

Tomatoes form the base of many a curry, and this sauce is a great foundation on which to build a curry by adding in your chosen meats, pulses and veg. Chicken or lamb go particularly well as do chickpeas (garbanzo beans). Courgettes (zucchini), squash and spinach are all equally good, although the latter is best added alongside something else. If you like a deeper tomato flavour, opt out of the coconut milk. However if you prefer a creamier curry, then the coconut milk is perfect.

SERVES 4

2 tablespoons sunflower or vegetable oil
1 onion, finely sliced
1 red chilli, finely sliced
Thumb-sized piece of fresh root ginger, finely grated (shredded)
3 garlic cloves, crushed or finely grated
2 tablespoons curry paste or powder (gluten-free, if necessary)
1 × 400-g (14-oz) tin chopped tomatoes
1 × 400-ml (14-fl oz) tin coconut milk (optional)

Heat the oil in a frying pan (skillet) over a gentle heat. Add the onion and fry for 8–10 minutes or until softened and beginning to brown.

Add the chilli, ginger and garlic, then cook for a few minutes. Stir in the curry paste or powder and cook for 1 minute.

Pour in the tinned tomatoes and half a tin of water or the coconut milk, if using. Simmer the sauce for 10 minutes to thicken a little.

Make it your way After cooking the onions, fry bite-sized pieces of your chosen meat until brown all over and then continue as instructed above. Once the tinned tomatoes and half a tin of water have been added, cook the curry for 10–15 minutes or until the meat is tender. For a veggie curry, pulses can be added in the same way as meat, but squash and courgettes (zucchini) are best cooked first and then stirred in for the final 10 minutes to ensure they cook without the sauce running dry. Spinach can be added in the last couple of minutes and cooked until wilted.

Tomato and Sage Pesto

Stirred through pasta, shaken into a dressing or dolloped on top of toast,
I absolutely love pesto. Sage is a natural companion to the tomatoes here.

SERVES 6–8

20 sage leaves, chopped
1 × 400-g (14-oz) tin chopped tomatoes
125g (4½oz) walnuts, chopped
Handful of parsley, roughly chopped
75g (2½oz) Parmesan or vegetarian
   Italian hard cheese, roughly chopped or
   grated (shredded)
4 garlic cloves, chopped
3 tablespoons olive oil
Juice of ½ lemon (optional)
Salt and freshly ground black pepper

Put all the ingredients except the lemon juice in a blender
with a good seasoning of salt and freshly ground black
pepper. Blitz to a coarse paste.

Taste and adjust the seasoning, if necessary. At this point
you can add more salt and pepper or squeeze in the lemon
juice. You can also add more or less sage and garlic
depending on your preference.

Zaalouk

Originating in Morocco, zaalouk is a popular salad, although we recognise it
as more of a dip. With aubergines (eggplants) at its heart, it's full of flavour.

SERVES 4–6 AS A DIP

2 aubergines (eggplants)
1 × 400-g (14-oz) tin chopped tomatoes
3 tablespoons olive oil
4 garlic cloves, crushed or finely grated
   (shredded)
2 teaspoons paprika
2 teaspoons ground cumin
⅛ teaspoon cayenne pepper
Handful of chopped parsley
Handful of chopped coriander (cilantro)
½ lemon

If you're cooking on gas, blister the skins of the aubergines
over the open flame. Alternatively, place them under the grill
(broiler). Once cool enough to handle, peel off the skins; you
can also cut the aubergine in half and scoop out the flesh.

Chop up the aubergine flesh and put into a frying pan
(skillet). Add the tinned tomatoes, 2 tablespoons oil, garlic,
spices and parsley to the pan, stir and cook for 10 minutes
over a gentle heat so the mixture is just simmering.

After the 10 minutes, cut the lemon into two wedges, tuck
one of the wedges into the mixture and cook for 5 minutes.

Remove the lemon wedge and spoon the zaalouk into a
serving bowl. Drizzle over the remaining oil, scatter over the
chopped coriander and squeeze over the juice from the
remaining lemon wedge.

Tomato Hummus

Is any gathering complete without hummus and crudités? Serving dips fills a host with confidence, knowing guests have something to nibble on, while guests are happy in the knowledge they have something to snack on before dinner. Here, tinned tomatoes bind everything together. With a cheerful light pink hue, their flavour brightens the hummus without being overpowering.

SERVES 4–6

1 × 227-g (8-oz) tin chopped tomatoes
1 × 400-g (14-oz) tin chickpeas
  (garbanzo beans), drained and rinsed
1 tablespoon tahini
1 tablespoon olive oil, plus extra
  for drizzling
½ teaspoon paprika, plus extra
  for garnishing
½ teaspoon ground cumin
1–2 garlic cloves, chopped
Handful of chopped parsley, plus a little
  extra for garnishing
Juice of ½ lemon
Salt and freshly ground black pepper

Put everything except the lemon juice into a food processor and blitz together until the chickpeas are roughly chopped.

Season well with salt and freshly ground black pepper, squeeze in a little lemon juice, blitz again and taste. If it needs more salt, pepper or lemon add it in and blitz again.

Spoon into a small serving bowl, drizzle on a little olive oil and scatter over some paprika and chopped parsley.

Try a twist If you want to add a little kick to this hummus, you can add a pinch or two of dried chilli flakes. If you like more of a Mediterranean flavour, swap out the parsley for basil. To intensify the tomato flavour, add a small handful of sun-dried tomatoes before blitzing.

Pan con Tomate

This classic tapas is traditionally made by rubbing toasted bread with a really ripe tomato, however, I love making it with good-quality tinned tomatoes. It makes a great lunch and is lush topped with ham, anchovies, cheese or simply a few torn basil leaves.

SERVES 2

1 ciabatta loaf
1 garlic clove
1 × 227-g (8-oz) tin polpa tomatoes
   (see tip below)
2 teaspoons extra virgin olive oil
Coarse sea salt flakes, to taste

Slice the ciabatta loaf in half lengthways. Toast the ciabatta halves under the grill (broiler) or in the toaster until golden on both sides.

Cut the garlic clove in half. Rub the cut side of the garlic clove over each slice of the toasted ciabatta. If you love garlic, push a little harder so you're almost using the toast as a grater.

Spoon over the tinned tomatoes, season with a pinch of sea salt and drizzle over the oil.

Cook's tip For this dish, I recommend buying the best quality chopped tomatoes you can afford. If you can find 'polpa' chopped tomatoes, these work really well. You may need to buy a 400-g (14-oz) tin – if so, that's the perfect excuse to make double. (Alternatively, use the leftover polpa tomatoes for another recipe.)

Loaded Nachos

What I love about loaded nachos is that you get to enjoy crispy nachos around the outside and then, as you eat closer towards the centre, they get a little softer. There's something for all tastes. Great for a movie night or a relaxed starter when entertaining, these nachos also work well with leftover chilli.

SERVES 2–4

1 × 200-g (7-oz) bag tortilla chips
1 × 227-g (8-oz) tin cherry tomatoes
1 small red onion, finely sliced
100g (3½oz) cooked chicken, pulled into shreds
Handful of sliced jalapeños from a jar
75g–100g (2½–3½oz) Cheddar cheese, grated (shredded)
75ml (2½fl oz) sour cream

Preheat the oven to 180°C/160°C fan/350°F/gas 4.

Scatter the tortilla chips over a roasting tray (sheet pan).

Drain the cherry tomatoes from the tin (the juices can always be used to make a Bloody Mary).

Spoon half the drained cherry tomatoes over the tortilla chips, then scatter over half the sliced red onion, half the shredded chicken and half the sliced jalapeños. Follow this with the remaining cherry tomatoes, red onion and chicken. Scatter over the cheese – I like to use the full 100g (3½oz), but 75g (2½oz) will do nicely.

Bake in the hot oven for 15–20 minutes or until the cheese has melted and is beginning to brown, but the nachos are not burnt.

Remove from the oven. Immediately before serving, spoon over the sour cream followed by the remaining jalapeños.

Green Beans with Tomato and Garlic

It's always handy to have a speedy side dish up your sleeve, even better when it's super simple but really flavourful. I love serving this alongside roast chicken or at a barbecue. It's also great cold so you can take it on a picnic, have it during the warmer months or eat the leftovers straight out of a container from the fridge. (And yes, I have done that.)

SERVES 4 AS A SIDE

500g (1lb 2oz) green beans, trimmed
2 teaspoons olive oil
2 shallots, finely chopped
3 garlic cloves, crushed
½ teaspoon paprika (optional)
1 × 227-g (8-oz) tin chopped tomatoes
2 teaspoons red wine vinegar
Handful of chopped parsley, to serve
  (optional)

Simmer the prepared green beans in salted boiling water (or steam them) for 3–4 minutes, until tender and still a vibrant green. Drain the beans, plunge them into cold water and then drain again. Set aside.

Heat the oil in a frying pan (skillet) and fry the shallots for 5 minutes until soft and lightly golden. Stir in the garlic and cook for 1 minute, then stir in the paprika, if using, and cook for 30 seconds. Pour in the tinned tomatoes and vinegar and cook for 5 minutes, simmering gently to thicken.

Tip in the cooked green beans and stir to coat well. Cook for 30 seconds to reheat the beans then serve. Alternatively, simply arrange the beans on a serving platter, spoon over the sauce and scatter over the chopped parsley.

Harissa Roasted Cauliflower

My friend Pauline introduced me to the idea of roasting cauliflower and since then I've roasted it every which way. It's heavenly roasted in oil with salt and pepper, but cauliflower has a way with flavour and happily shares its platform without losing its own qualities. Here I've gone for harissa because it goes so well with tomatoes and gives the florets a wonderful red hue. While the tinned tomatoes mean the cauliflower softens, they take this dish to the next level.

SERVES 2–4

3 tablespoons rose harissa paste
2 tablespoons olive oil
1 cauliflower, broken into florets and
    any large leaves halved
1 × 400-g (14-oz) tin chopped tomatoes
1 teaspoon ground cumin
Salt and freshly ground black pepper

Preheat the oven to 200°C/180°C fan/390°F/gas 6.

Combine the harissa paste and oil with a good helping of salt and freshly ground black pepper. Tip the cauliflower florets and leaves into a large bowl with the harissa mixture and toss (I usually use my hands) to ensure the cauliflower florets are well coated.

Tumble the cauliflower into a roasting tray (sheet pan) that is just big enough to hold it all. Roast in the hot oven for 30–40 minutes or until tender and crisping at the edges.

Meanwhile, open the tin of tomatoes and stir in the ground cumin with a pinch each of salt and pepper. Once the cauliflower is cooked, pour the tinned tomatoes over the top and carefully mix everything together so that all the florets are coated. Roast for a further 10–15 minutes or until the tomato sauce is piping hot.

Index

Cook's Index

Acknowledgements

I thought this would be the easiest part of writing a book, but so many people have got me to this point that compiling these acknowledgements has been difficult. Partly because I'm bound to forget someone, mostly because there aren't enough words to say everything I want to.

It's only polite to thank the team behind the book. These thanks aren't to be polite, they're heartfelt. Céline: thank you for your faith in me and being such good fun. Lisa (and of course Aubrey): thank you for keeping me on track, I feel very fortunate to have such a talented editor. Clare: the book is a visual stunner, so thank you. Mowie, Troy, Jess and Max: you all worked so hard to bring my recipes to life, thank you. I lucked out with the dream team.

There are a few other people without whom this book would not have happened. To Elly and Heather, thank you for believing in me and for your support and guidance. To Angela, your mentorship and advice has been transformational.

Before food writing, I had a career full of teachers and students who inspired me every day. To the CHS contingent — Ali, Charles, Dr C, Emma, Gill, Helen, Jill, Lou, M, Rach, Sarah, Sharon, Sue and Tara — thanks for keeping me sane all those years. To Jane and Emma W for the laughs. And to all the students. To Mrs May who not only inspired me to study food but also taught me to teach it.

Whatever you do in life, it's easier when you have people who believe in you. I was fortunate to have two early mentors, Orlando Murrin and Xanthe Clay, who were my champions, but are also good friends.

My food-writing journey began at an Arvon course, where I met a gang who turned into the best of friends who give me unwavering support. Thank you Katie, Kristen, Pauline, Rosie and Susan. I was also fortunate to meet so many encouraging people. Particular thanks go to Georgina, Karen, Les (and Liz) and Silvana for their kindness and advice.

To my Bath friends for tasting my early creations: Dan, Lesley, Max, Marilyn, Pete and Chloe. To Lindsey and Dave (and George and Violet), I'm sure Rapallo gave me most of my inspiration. To Kalpna for your endless support. To Nats for sorting me out every April. Thanks to the London lot: Bryony, Leo, Lucy, Ria and Rosie (chief tester). To Lindsay (and Ruby), thanks for being there when I need you and for all the Riesling. To Felicity (and Wilf) for the walks, moans and laughs. To Katie for the many cocktails. To Bex for sharing my love of the Spice Girls.

I'm lucky to work with super talented people. There are too many to mention but to the cookery team at GF — Ailsa, Anna, Barney, Cassie, Helena and Nadine — thank you for inspiring me and making every day a giggle. Thanks to Christine and Lulu for their support and guidance. Thanks to Keith and Janine for sharing their knowledge. Before GF I worked with fab people at TI/Future — thanks especially to the Lifestyle and Homes teams.

Thanks, too, to my colleagues and friends at the Guild of Food Writers, especially the committee and those who provided advice and ensured I had the time to work on the book. There are far too many to mention, but you know who you are.

For the York contingent — Lisa and Sam, Sarah (and Sue, of course) and Rob — who happily tested anything I cooked, especially Christmas in July.

Finally, and most importantly, to my family for always being there and allowing me to be whoever and whatever I wanted to be. To Gareth, my person, for testing everything I put in front of him. To Mum, Dad and Sarah, Nan and Grandad — my champions from the start. And to Ali and Dave, Will, Dan, Jean and Mike, Mel and Paul (and Gwenno) and Grace for all the encouragement, thank you. Thanks, too, to the Davies, Goldsmith and Whitworth clans — there are far too many to name. To Justin, although you're no longer here to see it, I know you'd be proud.